I Am Cute Dresses

25
SIMPLE
DESIGNS
TO SEW

Sato Watanabe

Copyright © 2006 Sato Watanabe

Japanese title: CHOKUSEN-NUI DE SUTEKI NA ONE PIECE
Originally published in Japanese language by Kawade Shobo Shinsha, Publishers
English translation rights arranged with Kawade Shobo Shinsha Publishers
through Timo Associates, Inc., Tokyo
Photograph: Takeshi Noguchi
Book Design: GRiD
Hair and Makeup: Zenji (apriru)
Illustration: Noriko Hachimonji, Mamiko Kobayashi
Pattern Design: Yumiko Yoshimoto

English-language rights, translation, and production by World Book Media, LLC
email info@worldbookmedia.com
English-language editor: Deborah Cannarella
English-language technical editor: Judith Durant
Translated by Asako Ohashi

First published in the United States in 2011 by Interweave Press

interweave.com
Interweave Press LLC
201 East 4th Street
Loveland, CO 80537-5655 USA
interweave.com

Cataloging-in-Publication data not available at time of printing
Printed in China

10 9 8 7 6 5 4 3 2 1

Contents

1
I Am Pleats
& Petals

This summer dress—with its open stand-up collar—is
right in style, every year. I chose a cotton-linen blend
fabric with a broad flower print along the selvedge
end. I laid out the pieces sideways on the fabric, so
the flowers bloom along the dress border. The wide
tuck pleats create a full and gently flowing skirt.

* fabric layout and how-to instructions → pp. 38–40

2

I Am Very V-Neck

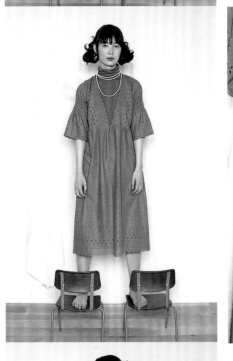

This sweet dress is made in an eyelet fabric with scalloped edges, which trim the dress front, sleeve ends, and hem. The shirring (the rows of decorative gathers on the upper sleeves) emphasizes the fullness of the sleeve ends and adds to the romantic charm. I like to wear this dress over a jersey turtleneck in a contrasting color.

* fabric layout and how-to instructions ➙ pp. 41–43

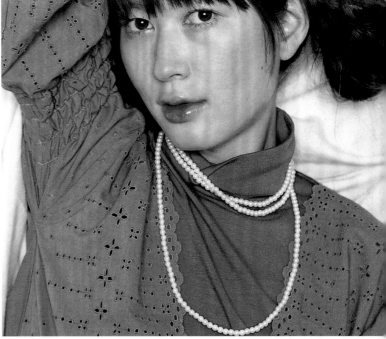

3 I Am Mandarin Empire

The pattern of the striped fabric, which is positioned vertically in the skirt and horizontally in the bodice, creates a feeling of both contrast and harmony at the same time. Accent the classic Mandarin collar with a contrasting leather or fabric ribbon, tied in a bow, for a lovely accent and neat finish.

* fabric layout and how-to instructions ➜ pp. 44–46

4 I Am Barely Ruffled

This dress, a variation of I Am Mandarin Empire, features frilly gathered ruffles around an open Mandarin collar. The sleeveless style, the loose fit, and the gently gathered skirt make this dress light and airy and comfortable to wear.

* fabric layout and how-to instructions ➜ pp. 47–49

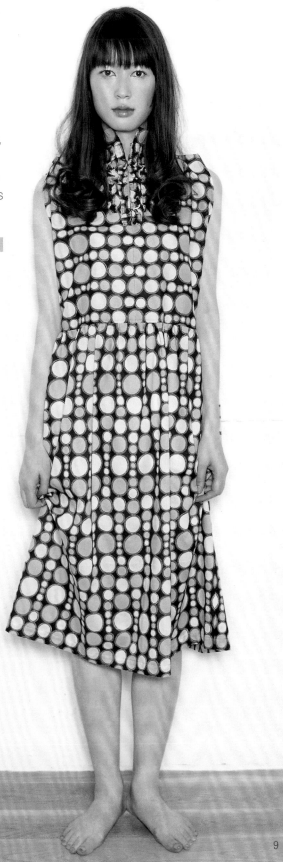

5 I Am Peekaboo Sleeves

This design transforms a simple square of fabric into an elegant one-piece dress. The top edge of each peekaboo sleeve is completely open, secured with only one button at the neckline edge and one at the sleeve end. The simple skirt is gathered with multiple rows of stitching at the waist and cinched with a drawstring ribbon. Wear this dress alone or, in cooler weather, with a pullover sweater or turtleneck underneath.

fabric layout and how-to instructions ➜ pp. 50–52

6

I Am Hello
Halter

This sexy summer dress has the classic appeal of the fashions you see in vintage Hollywood movies. The open-backed halter design will show off your beautiful back and shoulders. Make sure the waist fits snugly to emphasize your fabulous shape.

* fabric layout and how-to instructions ➜ pp. 53–55

7 I Am Simply Stand-Up

I fell in love with this oval-print fabric, which then gave me the idea to design a simple, clean, stylish dress. I created a truly straight silhouette with a fluid line that flows from collar to hem. The welts on each pocket opening add a unique fashion detail. The skirt is made of eight panels of equal size, cut into trapezoids.

* fabric layout and how-to instructions → pp. 56–59

8 I Am Baby Bateau

Here's another simple dress to make with a fabric you love. It's a variation of I Am Simply Stand-Up, but this dress has a straight, open, boatneck-style neckline instead. It also has a longer finished length. I always love wearing this dress because the long, flowing line makes me look tall and thin.

* fabric layout and how-to instructions → pp. 60–63

13

9 I Am Sassy Sundress

This dress is full of playful charm. The gathered waist and irregular hemline creates airy volume in the swinging folds of the skirt. Imagine the visual effect of all that movement if you made the dress in a striped or patterned fabric.

* fabric layout and how-to instructions → pp.64–68

10

I Am
Twice
As Nice

Fabrics really speak to me. I think it was love at first sight when I found this elegant floral print. This sleeveless, two-toned dress will take you anywhere you want to go. It's casual and fun, making it perfect for daytime. It's also dramatic and graceful enough for evening.

* fabric layout and how-to instructions ➜ pp. 69–71

11 I Am
Tiny
Tucks

With just the simplest details, a square of fabric becomes this dramatic dress with lovely beaded puff sleeves. The few beads, handstitched across the bodice and armhole openings, elevate this dress to the status of haute couture. The silhouette is slimming, thanks to the darts at the high waistline.

fabric layout and how-to instructions → pp. 72–75

12

I Am Raglan to Riches

This tartan-plaid fabric and torchon lace trim make a surprising and superb combination. The dress has a square neckline and a raglan-style French sleeve. You can wear it year-round as is or as a jumper with a warm pullover or jersey turtleneck underneath.

* fabric layout and how-to instructions ➜ pp. 76–78

13

I Am All the Trimmings

Wide gathered ruffles flow along the edges of the neckline and hem of this dress. Elastic tape stitched at the sleeve ends creates the effect of ruffles at the wrists. You can wear this garment as a dress or over pants or leggings. If you make the same pattern in a lightweight cotton or silky fabric, it becomes a princess-style nightie.

* fabric layout and how-to instructions ➜ pp. 79–81

14 I Am All Wrapped Up

This dress is a must-have addition to your wardrobe. It's flattering, versatile, and comfortable to wear. Instead of closing the dress with a ribbon tie, you can finish the side seam with a button or another type of closure.

fabric layout and how-to instructions → pp. 82–85

15

I Am
Dainty
Drops

A seersucker dress—light and airy—is essential for summertime. The loose fit of this design and the low drop waistline gives this dress a youthful, sweet, and elegant style. Gentle shirring at the shoulders creates a soft sleeve silhouette that follows and flatters the shape of your arms.

* fabric layout and how-to instructions → pp. 86–88

16 I Am Cute Contrast

The vibrant colors of this striped Italian linen really make the most of this design. The horizontal strip at the hem mirrors the horizontal stripes on the bodice to create a wonderful effect. Linen, which has a firm texture, is a perfect fabric choice because it holds the shape of the skirt's simply tacked box pleats.

fabric layout and how-to instructions ➜ pp. 89–91

17

I Am
Sweetly
Tied

I finally found just the way to showcase the
lovely floral print fabric I've been saving in my
closet for fifteen years! This design is similar to
I Am Twice As Nice. Both dresses have a
simple tuck at center front, but each has
a unique look. This dress also has
a shorter finished length. Make
this everyday dress in a fabric
that has a lot of drape to
guarantee a slimming
silhouette.

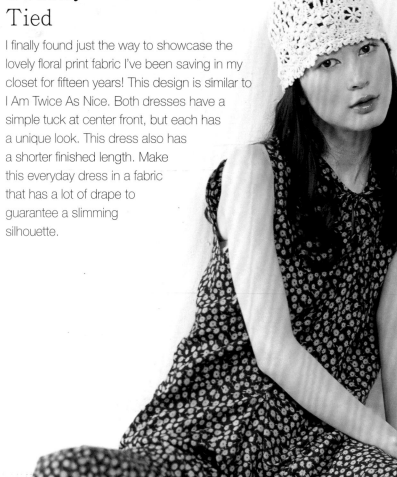

* fabric layout and how-to instructions ➜ pp. 92–93

18 I Am Tripled Tier

This design combines the fashion and appeal of the popular tiered skirt with the comfort and ease of a one-piece dress. It's both hip and sweet at the same time. The dobby voile fabric is trimmed with black cotton lace. You can easily adjust the length by adding or subtracting tiers of ruffles.

* fabric layout and how-to instructions ➜ pp. 94–97

19

I Am
Jumper
for Joy

I really love big cargo pockets, especially when combined with simple skirts and dresses. They really make a statement! I made this everyday black jumper with machine-washable 100-percent nylon—to ensure I'll get a lot of use out of it. For a more elegant look, I made the same dress out of a gray twill fabric (shown on page 25).

Just by changing materials, you can change the entire look of the design. That's the real thrill of sewing for yourself. Pick your favorite design and make two or three dresses with different fabrics to create a variety of effects. A flower print would work well for this style, too!

* fabric layout and how-to instructions → pp. 98–101

* fabric layout and how-to instructions → pp. 102–105

20

I Am Sew Buttoned Down

The slightly irregular placement of the buttonholes and buttons on the top front of this dress creates an unusual design detail. Because this feature is sure to catch the eye, the buttons you choose are key. The wide ruffle at the hem of the long skirt provides another showy detail.

21
I Am Shift into Tunic

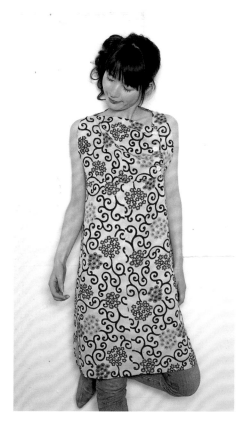

I received some lovely kimono cloth as a gift and turned it into this charming dress. I loved the fabric's combination of bold pattern and beautiful colors.

A Japanese kimono is a simple garment with straight lines, like all of the designs in this book, and so is this fantastic knee-length dress, which can also be worn as a tunic top over pants or leggings.

* fabric layout and how-to instructions ➜ pp. 106–108

22 I Am Magical Insets

The simple straight lines of this design are perfectly suited for unstructured, draping dolman sleeves. The elegant French lace plays the leading role in this garment and creates an unforgettable, one-of-a-kind look. You could also substitute tiers of narrow widths of lace to create the same effect at the bodice and sleeve ends.

fabric layout and how-to instructions → pp. 109–110

23 I Am Kimono Cut

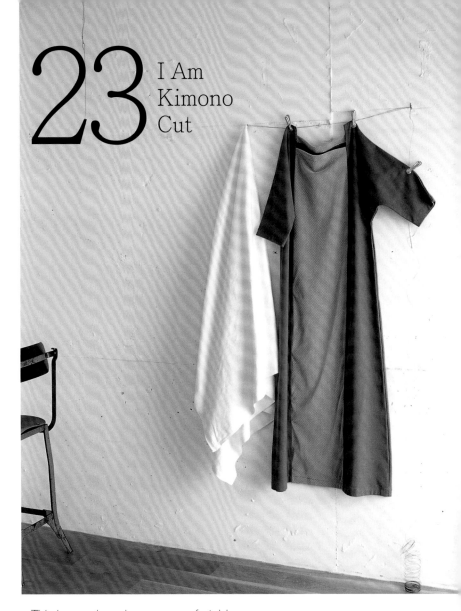

This jersey dress is super-comfortable and easy to wear. The center front and back panels of the dress shown here are covered with dotted tulle. You could also make the center panels in a strongly contrasting color or print fabric. The sleeve ends and the seams joining the front panel and dress sides are stitched with a decorative zigzag stitch.

* fabric layout and how-to instructions ➜ pp. 111–112

24

I Am
Box-Pleated
Wonder

This dress is a classic style, accented with
two rows of decorative buttons and loops.
The loose fit makes the dress easy to slip
on over your head, but you could add a
closure at the seam if you prefer. There are
three inverted box pleats on the skirt—two
in the front and one at center back.

*fabric layout and how-to instructions ➜ pp. 113–117

25

I Am Satin Doll

This gorgeous little dress has lace applied to the bodice and to alternate skirt panels. It also has faux fur stitched to the camisole dress straps. You could decorate the straps with lace instead. The dress is so cute, you could even omit the strap embellishment altogether. (See the Contents page for a view of the simpler style.)

fabric layout and how-to instructions ➜ pp. 118–120

Construction Tips

All the dresses featured in this book are simple shapes, designed to be loose-fitting, one-size-fits-all garments. The dresses are intended to fit a range of sizes. The dimensions given assume an average bust measurement of 35–36 inches and an average hip measurement of 38–39 inches. Some designs include formulas (marked with black stars) that will help you adjust the width of the garment to fit your own body measurements.

Adjust the length of each dress to the length you prefer simply by raising or dropping the hemline. If you have a dress that you love the fit and length of, you can simply measure that garment and cut the fabric pieces to the same approximate length—both from shoulder to waist or hip and from shoulder to hem.

Keep in mind that the measurements noted in inches on the patterns are rounded conversions of the metric measurements. For the most accurate fit, use the metric version of all measurements and sizing adjustments. Some common pattern construction symbols are shown on page 36.

Usually, when you're making garments, fitting the flat fabrics on your three-dimensional body can be challenging. One of the best features of straight-stitching simple shapes is the speedy tailoring! So enjoy making—and wearing—your easy-to-sew and easy-to-fit dresses.

Let's get started!

Basic Techniques

Zigzag-Stitching Seam Allowances

Stitch length approx. 1/16" (0.2cm)

Stitch width, approx 1/8" (0.3cm)

Stitches should overhang raw edges of fabric.

This seam allowance finish works well on tightly woven fabrics. You can also finish the raw edges with a serger if you have one.

Making a Single-Fold Hem

Zigzag-stitched or serged raw edge

1/4" (0.5cm)

First zigzag-stitch or serge the raw edge of the fabric. Then fold under the hem and stitch in place.

Serging Seam Allowances

Excess seam allowance, approx. 1/4" (0.5cm)

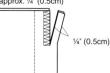

1/4" (0.5cm)

Join fabrics with dense stitch. In some cases, allow extra seam allowance width because the serger stitches and cuts at the same time.

Making a Two-Fold Hem

1/16" (0.2cm)

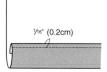

Fold fabric twice and stitch. This folded hem can range in width from as narrow as 1/8" to 1/4" (0.3 to 0.5cm) to as wide as 1 1/2" (4cm). Two-fold hemming can also be used as an edge finish.

Joining Bias Strips

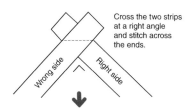

Cross the two strips at a right angle and stitch across the ends.

Wrong side

Right side

1/4" (0.5cm)

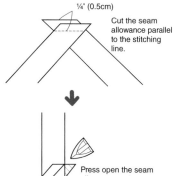

Cut the seam allowance parallel to the stitching line.

Press open the seam allowance and remove the excess overhanging the sides of the strip.

Wrong side

• Pattern Construction Symbols

Outline and stitching line

Facing edge

Fabric fold

Multiple sections
This symbol indicates two or more garment sections in the fabric width or length.

Notch mark
Join notch marks precisely in order to keep the rest of the seam open.

Edge-to-edge positioning
Position paper patterns edge to edge before cutting.

Right angle
This symbol indicates that the marked area should form a 90-degree angle.

Tucking
The downward direction of the diagonal line indicates the direction of the tuck. This drawing indicates the tuck is folded from left to right.

Fabric grain line
The direction of the arrow indicates the direction of the warp threads.

Glossary

Backing: An interfacing is often attached to the wrong side of the fashion fabric to reinforce, stiffen, or add thickness to the fabric. The interfacing is always a different weight and type of fabric than the fashion fabric for the dress.

Bust measurement: The bust measurement is the measurement around the fullest part of the bust.

Dart: A dart is a fold sewn into the garment to shape flat fabric pieces so that they conform to the shape of a three-dimensional body.

Dolman sleeve: This term refers to a style of sleeve that is formed as one piece with the body of the garment. It creates a loose-fitting arm opening that doesn't have a seam where the sleeve meets the body. The name comes from a Turkish overcoat that traditionally had this characteristic style of sleeve.

Ease: Ease is the extra amount of fabric beyond the body's exact measurements that provides wearing comfort in a garment.

Hip measurement: The hip measurement is the measurement around the fullest part of the hips.

Invisible zipper: An invisible zipper is hidden, because its teeth are covered when it's closed. Because this type of closure is "invisible," it does not interfere with the finished appearance of the garment.

Right side of fabric: The right side of the fabric is the side that will be visible when you are wearing the garment.

Selvedge: The selvedge is the finished edge on each side of a woven fabric, which prevents raveling.

Shirring: This technique is a type of gathering method that allows you to create three-dimensional effects in your garments. To shirr fabric, you simply tension the bobbin thread of the machine (usually an elastic, cotton thread), as shown on page 42.

Support button: To reinforce a closure while also neatly covering a knotted thread end, simply attach a tiny, support button on the inside of the garment directly behind the outside button that is the primary fastener.

Tiers: To add fullness and flair to the body of a skirt, create tiers of fabric by stitching two or three ruffles or panels to the bottom portion of the garment.

Tucks: Tucks are a type of fold that provides another way to create structure in the surface and silhouette of a garment. Both for ease and for appearance, tucks are not stitched along their length. They are only stitched at top and fall into a gentle, flowing shape in the skirt of a dress.

Waist measurement: The waist measurement is the measurement of the body between the bottom of the rib cage and the top of the hip bones. It is usually the narrowest part of the body.

Wrong side of fabric: The wrong side of the fabric is the side that will be concealed on the inside of the garment.

1 I Am Pleats & Petals
(shown on pages 4–5)

Materials

Fabric: 114¼" x 44" (290 cm x 112 cm) of floral border-print fabric

Fusible interfacing: 19¾" x 8" (50 cm x 20 cm)

Invisible zipper: 28" (71 cm)

Hook and eye: 1 set

Optional Sizing Adjustments

For the most accurate fit, use the metric version of all measurements and sizing adjustments.

★ a = H / 4 + 13 ¾" (35 cm)

★ b = H / 4 + 11¾" (30 cm)

★ c = H / 4

★ d =H / 16

H = Finished hip measurement

Seam Allowances

Unless otherwise noted, seam allowances are ⅜" (1 cm).

● **Fabric Layout**

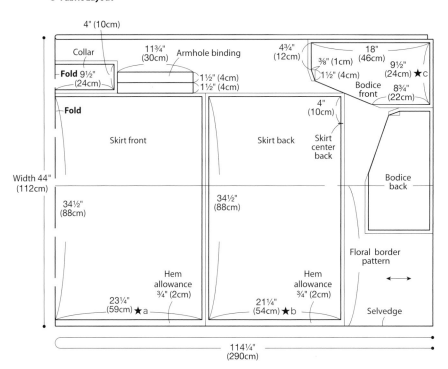

Construction Steps

1. Enclose raw edges of armholes on bodice front and back with folded fabric binding and stitch.

2. Stitch bodice front pieces at center front. Topstitch ¼" (½ cm) from stitching line.

3. Stitch bodice fronts and backs together at shoulder and side seams.

4. Attach fusible interfacing to entire width of wrong side of collar. Stitch collar to neck opening right sides together, as shown (A).

5. Fold pleats in skirt front and two skirt back panels, as shown (B). Stitch the skirt at sides and center back.

6. Stitch the skirt to the body. Topstitch ¼" (½ cm) from the stitching line.

7. Install the zipper at center back as shown on page 74. Finish the top of the zipper by folding the tape to the wrong side at center back and blindstitching (C).

8. Hem the skirt with a ¾" (2 cm) hem.

9. Attach the hook-and-eye closure to the center back of the collar as shown on page 59.

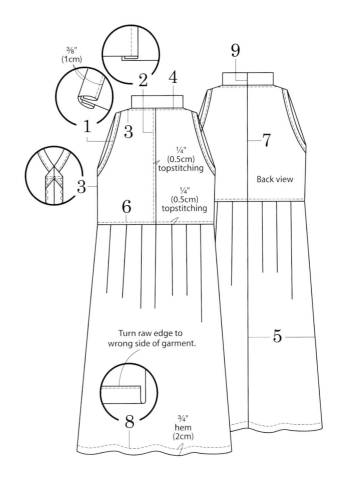

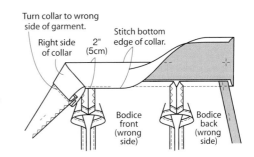

A. Attaching the Collar

Shoulder seam

Collar (right side)

Back (wrong side)   Front (wrong side)

Attach fusible interfacing to wrong side of entire collar. Join collar and front body, right sides together.

Turn collar to wrong side of garment.

Stitch bottom edge of collar.

Right side of collar   2" (5cm)

Bodice front (wrong side)   Bodice back (wrong side)

B. Positioning and Folding the Pleats

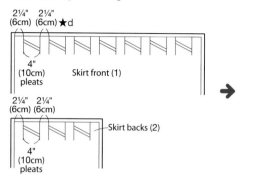

2¼" (6cm) 2¼" (6cm) ★d

4" (10cm) pleats Skirt front (1)

2¼" (6cm) 2¼" (6cm)

Skirt backs (2)

4" (10cm) pleats

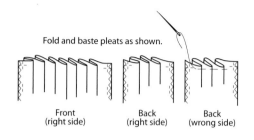

Fold and baste pleats as shown.

Front (right side) Back (right side) Back (wrong side)

C. Finishing the Zipper

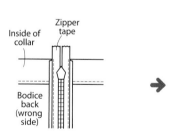

Inside of collar Zipper tape

Bodice back (wrong side)

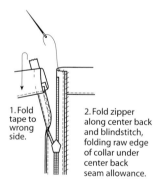

1. Fold tape to wrong side.

2. Fold zipper along center back and blindstitch, folding raw edge of collar under center back seam allowance.

2 I Am Very V-Neck

(shown on pages 6–7)

Materials

Fabric: 126" x 41" (320 cm x 104 cm) of scallop-edged eyelet fabric

Elastic thread for bobbin (for shirring)

Optional Sizing Adjustments

For the most accurate fit, use the metric version of all measurements and sizing adjustments.

★ a = B / 4

★ b = B / 2

B = Finished bust measurement

Seam Allowances

Unless otherwise noted, seam allowances are ⅜" (1 cm).

● **Fabric Layout**

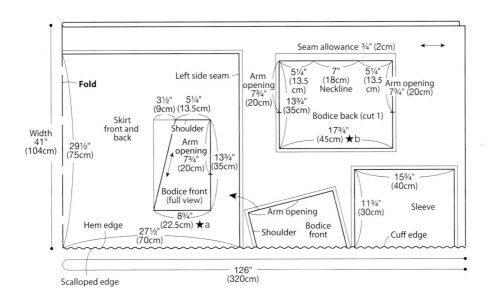

Construction Steps

1. Stitch shoulder seams. Turn under raw edge along rear neckline and stitch (A).

2. Attach the sleeves to the bodice. Stitch five rows of shirring stitches, spaced ¾" (2 cm) apart (B).

3. Stitch bodice side seams and underarm seams (C).

4. Stitch left skirt side seam and press open.

5. Gather waist and stitch to bodice. Then topstitch.

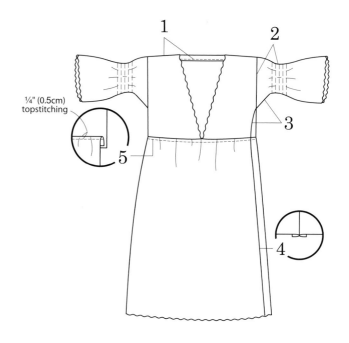

¼" (0.5cm)
topstitching

● **Shirring the Sleeves**

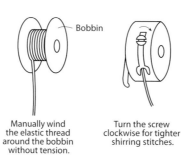

Manually wind
the elastic thread
around the bobbin
without tension.

Turn the screw
clockwise for tighter
shirring stitches.

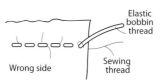

Elastic
bobbin
thread

Wrong side

Sewing
thread

Test the stitching on scrap fabric. Shirr the fabric to
reduce width from 15¾" (40cm) to 9¾" (25cm).

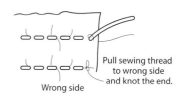

Pull sewing thread
to wrong side
and knot the end.

Wrong side

A. Stitching the Shoulder and Neckline

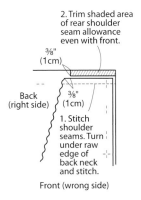

2. Trim shaded area of rear shoulder seam allowance even with front.

⅜" (1cm)

Back (right side)

⅜" (1cm)

1. Stitch shoulder seams. Turn under raw edge of back neck and stitch.

Front (wrong side)

B. Attaching the Sleeves

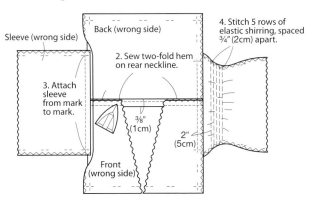

Sleeve (wrong side)

Back (wrong side)

4. Stitch 5 rows of elastic shirring, spaced ¾" (2cm) apart.

2. Sew two-fold hem on rear neckline.

3. Attach sleeve from mark to mark.

⅜" (1cm)

2" (5cm)

Front (wrong side)

1. Join shoulder seam allowances with zigzag stitch and press toward back.

C. Stitching Side and Underarm Seams

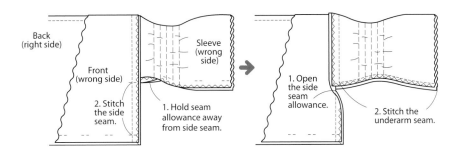

Back (right side)

Sleeve (wrong side)

Front (wrong side)

2. Stitch the side seam.

1. Hold seam allowance away from side seam.

1. Open the side seam allowance.

2. Stitch the underarm seam.

3 I Am Mandarin Empire

(shown on page 8)

Materials

Fabric: 94½" x 44¾" (240 cm x 114 cm) of glitter-printed cord lawn

Fusible interfacing: 18" x 3" (46 cm x 8 cm)

Leather tape: 53" (135 cm) of ⅛" (0.4 cm) tape

Optional Sizing Adjustments

For the most accurate fit, use the metric version of all measurements and sizing adjustments.

★ a = H / 4

H = Finished hip measurement

Seam Allowances

Unless otherwise noted, seam allowances are ⅜" (1 cm).

● **Fabric Layout**

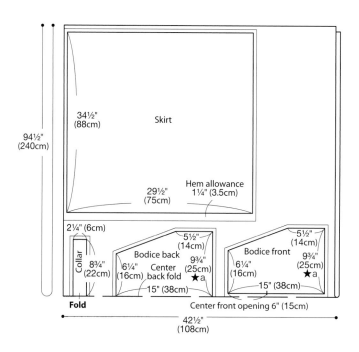

Construction Steps

1. Make the collar (A).

2. Stitch the shoulder seams (B).

3. Attach the collar (C).

4. Stitch the side seams and neckline (D).

5. Stitch the center front seam of the bodice and finish center opening (E).

6. Stitch the side seams of the skirt. Gather the skirt (F).

7. Attach the skirt to the bodice at the waistline. Topstitch.

8. Hem the dress with a ¾" (2 cm) hem, turning under ¼" (0.5 cm) of raw edge.

9. Attach the leather tape as a tie closure at the open neckline.

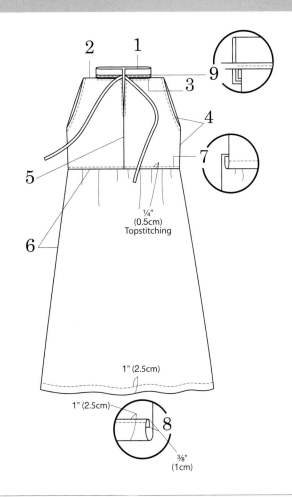

¼"
(0.5cm)
Topstitching

1" (2.5cm)

1" (2.5cm)

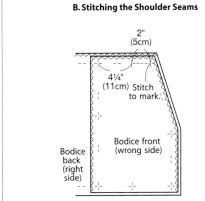

⅜"
(1cm)

A. Making the Collar

Attach fusible interfacing to entire wrong side.

Collar (wrong side)

1. Fold the collar lengthwise, right sides together.

2. Stitch end. 3. Stitch end.

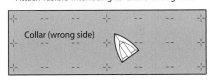

Collar (right side)

Turn collar to right side and zigzag-stitch raw edges together.

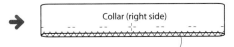

B. Stitching the Shoulder Seams

2"
(5cm)

4¼"
(11cm) Stitch to mark.

Bodice front
(wrong side)

Bodice back
(right side)

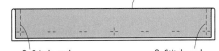

C. Attaching the Collar

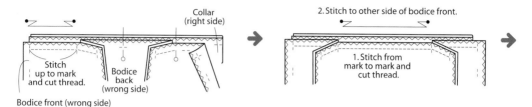

Collar (right side)

Stitch up to mark and cut thread.

Bodice back (wrong side)

Bodice front (wrong side)

2. Stitch to other side of bodice front.

1. Stitch from mark to mark and cut thread.

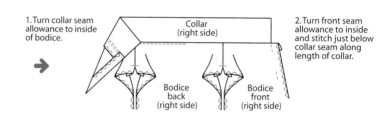

1. Turn collar seam allowance to inside of bodice.

Collar (right side)

2. Turn front seam allowance to inside and stitch just below collar seam along length of collar.

Bodice back (right side)

Bodice front (right side)

D. Finishing Side Seams and Neckline

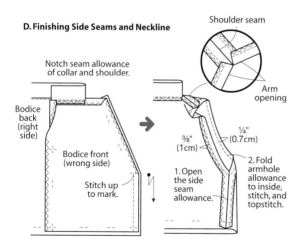

Shoulder seam

Notch seam allowance of collar and shoulder.

Arm opening

Bodice back (right side)

Bodice front (wrong side)

Stitch up to mark.

3/8" (1cm)

1/4" (0.7cm)

1. Open the side seam allowance.

2. Fold armhole allowance to inside, stitch, and topstitch.

E. Stitching Bodice Front

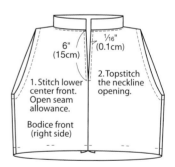

6" (15cm)

1/16" (0.1cm)

1. Stitch lower center front. Open seam allowance.

2. Topstitch the neckline opening.

Bodice front (right side)

F. Stitching and Gathering Skirt

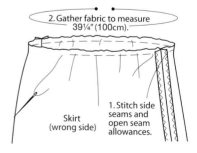

2. Gather fabric to measure 39¼" (100cm).

Skirt (wrong side)

1. Stitch side seams and open seam allowances.

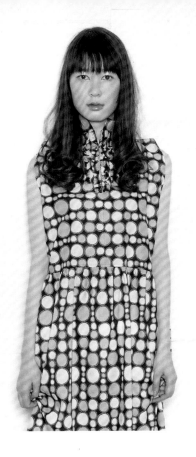

4 I Am Barely Ruffled

(shown on page 9)

Materials

Fabric: 78¾" x 42½" (200 cm x 114 cm) of silky printed lawn

Fusible interfacing: 18" x 3" (46 cm x 8 cm)

Hook and eye: 1 set

Optional Sizing Adjustments

For the most accurate fit, use the metric version of all measurements and sizing adjustments.

★ a = H / 4

H = Finished hip measurement

Seam Allowances

Unless otherwise noted, seam allowances are ⅜" (1 cm).

● **Making Ruffles**

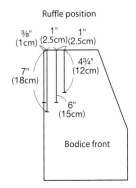

Ruffle position

⅜" (1cm)   1" (2.5cm)   1" (2.5cm)

7" (18cm)   4¾" (12cm)

6" (15cm)

Bodice front

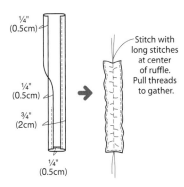

¼" (0.5cm)

¼" (0.5cm)

¾" (2cm)

¼" (0.5cm)

Stitch with long stitches at center of ruffle. Pull threads to gather.

● **Fabric Layout**

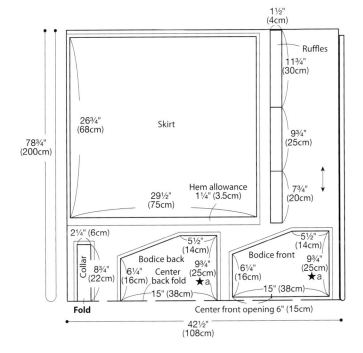

1½" (4cm)

Ruffles

11¾" (30cm)

26¾" (68cm)   Skirt

9¾" (25cm)

78¾" (200cm)

7¾" (20cm)

Hem allowance 1¼" (3.5cm)

29½" (75cm)

2¼" (6cm)

5½" (14cm)

5½" (14cm)

Bodice back

Collar

8¾" (22cm)

6¼" (16cm)

Center back fold

9¾" (25cm) ★a

Bodice front

6¼" (16cm)

9¾" (25cm) ★a

15" (38cm)

15" (38cm)

Fold

Center front opening 6" (15cm)

42½" (108cm)

Construction Steps

1. Attach the six ruffles (A).

2. Make the collar (B).

3. Stitch the shoulder seams (C).

4. Attach the collar (D).

5. Stitch the side seams and finish the neckline (E).

6. Stitch the center front seam of the bodice and finish center opening (F).

7. Stitch the side seams of the skirt. Gather the skirt (G).

8. Attach the skirt to the bodice at the waistline. Topstitch.

9. Hem the dress with a ¾" (2 cm) hem, turning under ¼" (0.5 cm) of raw edge.

10. Attach the hook-and-eye closure to the center back of the collar as shown on page 59.

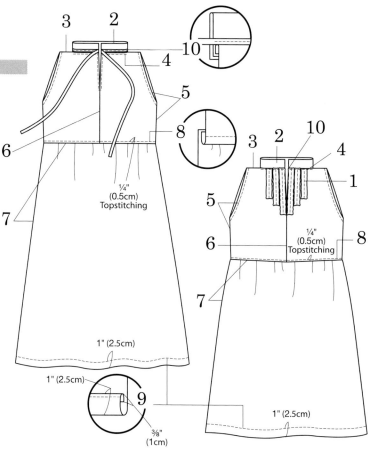

A. Attaching the Ruffles

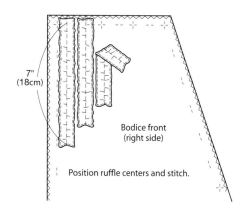

7" (18cm)

Bodice front (right side)

Position ruffle centers and stitch.

Full length to gathered length:
11¾" to 7" (30cm to 18cm)
9¾" to 6" (25cm to 15cm)
8" to 4¾" (20cm to 12cm)

B. Making the Collar

Attach fusible interfacing to entire wrong side.

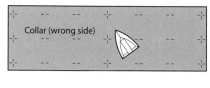

Collar (wrong side)

1. Fold the collar lengthwise, right sides together.

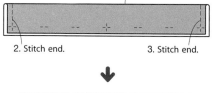

2. Stitch end.   3. Stitch end.

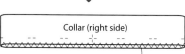

Collar (right side)

Turn collar to right side and zigzag-stitch raw edges together.

C. Stitching the Shoulder Seams

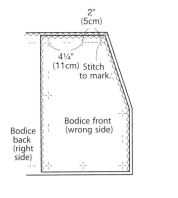

2"
(5cm)

4¼"
(11cm) Stitch
to mark.

Bodice front
(wrong side)

Bodice
back
(right
side)

D. Attaching the Collar

Collar
(right side)

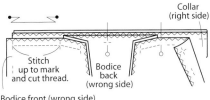

Stitch
up to mark
and cut thread.

Bodice
back
(wrong side)

Bodice front (wrong side)

2. Stitch to other side of bodice front.

1. Stitch from
mark to mark and
cut thread.

1. Turn collar seam
allowance to inside
of bodice.

2. Turn front seam
allowance to inside
and stitch just below
collar seam along
length of collar.

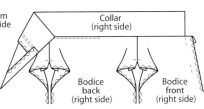

Collar
(right side)

Bodice
back
(right side)

Bodice
front
(right side)

E. Finishing Side Seams and Neckline

Shoulder seam

Notch seam allowance
of collar and shoulder.

Arm
opening

Bodice
back
(right
side)

Bodice front
(wrong side)

Stitch up
to mark.

1. Open
the side
seam
allowance.

3⁄8"
(1cm)

¼"
(0.7cm)

2. Fold
armhole
allowance
to inside,
stitch, and
topstitch.

F. Stitching Bodice Front

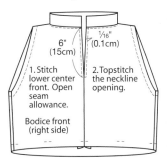

6"
(15cm)

1⁄16"
(0.1cm)

1. Stitch
lower center
front. Open
seam
allowance.

2. Topstitch
the neckline
opening.

Bodice front
(right side)

G. Stitching and Gathering Skirt

2. Gather fabric to measure
39¼" (100cm).

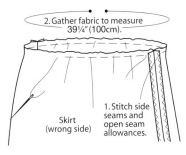

Skirt
(wrong side)

1. Stitch side
seams and
open seam
allowances.

5 I Am Peekaboo Sleeves

(shown on page 10)

Materials

Fabric: 90½" x 42½" (230 cm x 108 cm) of stone-washed linen chambray

Fusible interfacing: Two pieces, ¾" x 1½" (2 cm x 4 cm)

Elastic tape: 86¾" (220 cm) length of ⅜" (1 cm) tape

Buttons: 10 matching, with ⅝" (1.5 cm) diameter

Optional Sizing Adjustments

For the most accurate fit, use the metric version of all measurements and sizing adjustments.

Seam Allowances

Unless otherwise noted, seam allowances are ⅜" (1 cm).

● **Fabric Layout**

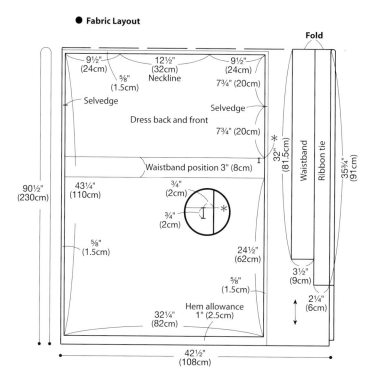

Construction Steps

1. Stitch the right side seam. Make the drawstring casing and apply to dress at waistline (A).

2. Insert elastic tape in casing. Stitch left side seam and shoulder. Turn under ¼" (0.5 cm) of raw edge and stitch ¾" (2 cm) hem (B).

3. Finish the neckline, the shoulder, and the sleeve hems (C).

4. Make the ribbon tie for the waist and feed it into the drawstring casing.

5. Sew three buttons onto the end of each tie. Sew two buttons along the top of each sleeve.

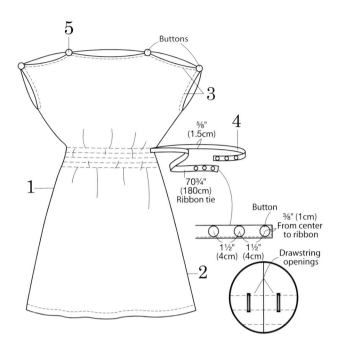

A. Making the Drawstring Waistband

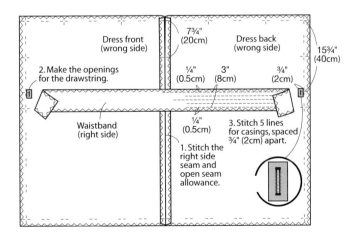

B. Stitching Left Side Seam, Shoulders, and Hems

3. Stitch in 4 places, as marked, along the top shoulder and neckline.

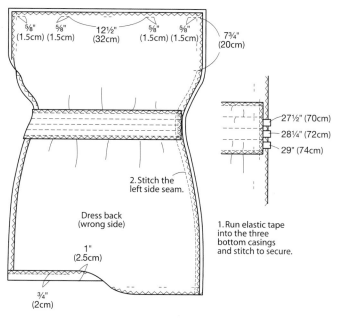

⅝" (1.5cm)   ⅝" (1.5cm)   12½" (32cm)   ⅝" (1.5cm)   ⅝" (1.5cm)   7¾" (20cm)

27½" (70cm)
28¼" (72cm)
29" (74cm)

2. Stitch the left side seam.

Dress back (wrong side)

1. Run elastic tape into the three bottom casings and stitch to secure.

1" (2.5cm)

¾" (2cm)

4. To finish, fold the hem, turning under the raw edge ¼" (0.5cm), and stitch.

C. Finishing the Neckline, Shoulder, and Sleeve Hems

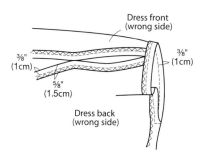

Dress front (wrong side)

⅜" (1cm)   ⅜" (1cm)

⅝" (1.5cm)

Dress back (wrong side)

6 I Am Hello Halter

(shown on page 11)

Materials

Fabric: 94½" x 45¾" (240 cm x 116 cm) of polka-dot-print fabric

Fusible interfacing: 31½" x 11¾" (80 cm x 30 cm)

Invisible zipper: 13¾" (35 cm) long

Hook and eye: 1 set

Optional Sizing Adjustments

For the most accurate fit, use the metric version of all measurements and sizing adjustments.

★ a =½ finished underbust measurement

Seam Allowances

Unless otherwise noted, seam allowances are ⅜" (1 cm).

● **Fabric Layout**

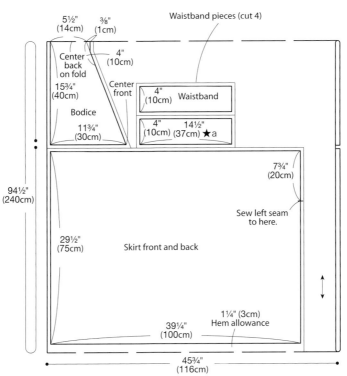

Construction Steps

1. Assemble and gather the bodice (A).

2. Attach waistband to bodice (B).

3. Stitch right seam of skirt and press open seam allowance. Join waistband and skirt (C).

4. Stitch left seam of skirt and press open the seam allowance (D).

5. Attach the invisible zipper as shown on page 74.

6. Finish the waistband, turning under raw edges (E). Topstitch. Stitch hem.

7. Attach the hook-and-eye closure to the waistband as shown on page 59.

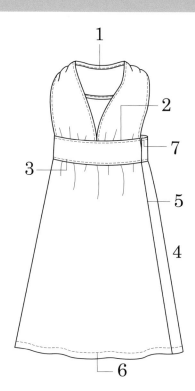

A. Gathering the Bodice

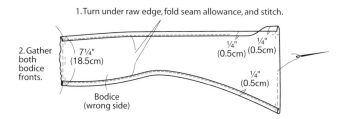

1. Turn under raw edge, fold seam allowance, and stitch.

2. Gather both bodice fronts.

7¼"
(18.5cm)

¼"
(0.5cm)

¼"
(0.5cm)

¼"
(0.5cm)

Bodice
(wrong side)

B. Attaching the Waistband

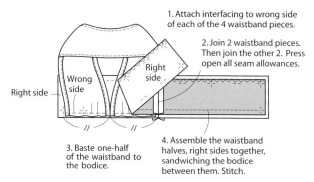

1. Attach interfacing to wrong side of each of the 4 waistband pieces.

2. Join 2 waistband pieces. Then join the other 2. Press open all seam allowances.

Right side

Wrong side

Right side

3. Baste one-half of the waistband to the bodice.

4. Assemble the waistband halves, right sides together, sandwiching the bodice between them. Stitch.

C. Assembling the Bodice and Skirt

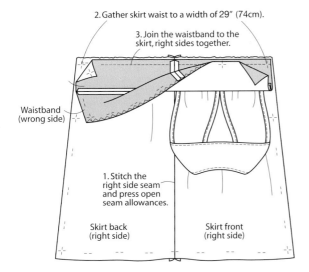

2. Gather skirt waist to a width of 29″ (74cm).

3. Join the waistband to the skirt, right sides together.

Waistband (wrong side)

1. Stitch the right side seam and press open seam allowances.

Skirt back (right side)

Skirt front (right side)

D. Stitching the Left Side Seam

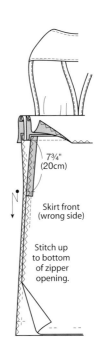

7¾″ (20cm)

Skirt front (wrong side)

Stitch up to bottom of zipper opening.

E. Finishing the Waistband and Hem

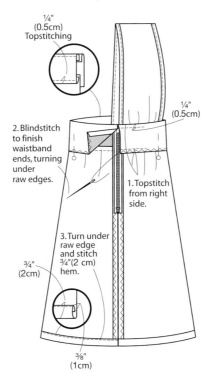

¼″ (0.5cm) Topstitching

¼″ (0.5cm)

2. Blindstitch to finish waistband ends, turning under raw edges.

1. Topstitch from right side.

3. Turn under raw edge and stitch ¾″ (2 cm) hem.

¾″ (2cm)

⅜″ (1cm)

7 I Am Simply Stand-Up

(shown on pages 12–13)

Materials

Fabric: 55" x 56" (140 cm x 142 cm) of printed cotton-linen blend

Fusible interfacing: 19¾" x 7¾" (50 cm x 20 cm)

Invisible zipper: 27½" (70 cm) long

Hook and eye: 1 set

Optional Sizing Adjustments

For the most accurate fit, use the metric version of all measurements and sizing adjustments.

★ a = H / 16

★ b = H / 16 + 1½" (4 cm)

★ c = H / 4

★ d = H / 8

Seam Allowances

Unless otherwise noted, seam allowances are ⅜" (1 cm).

● **Fabric Layout**

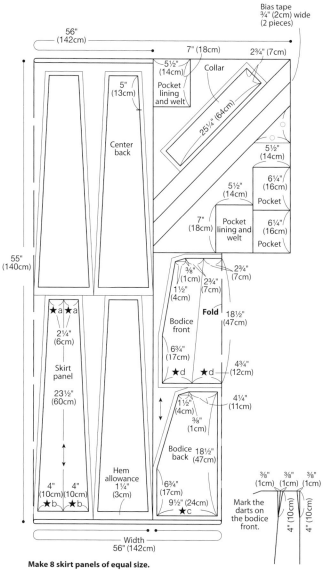

Make 8 skirt panels of equal size.

Construction Steps

1. Stitch darts in bodice pieces (A).

2. Make the two pockets (B).

3. Finish the neckline and armholes (C).

4. Stitch the shoulder seams and press. Attach the collar as shown on page 39. Stitch the bodice side seams and press open seam allowances (D).

5. Zigzag-stitch the raw edges of the skirt panels. Join the four skirt front panels. Join the two right back panels of the skirt. Then join the two left back panels of the skirt. Press open all of the seam allowances.

6. Stitch the center back up to the zipper opening.

7. Stitch the skirt side seams and press open the seam allowances.

8. Attach the skirt to the bodice. Topstitch.

9. Install the invisible zipper as shown on page 74.

10. Sew the hem, zigzag-stitching the raw edge.

11. Attach the hook-and-eye closure (E).

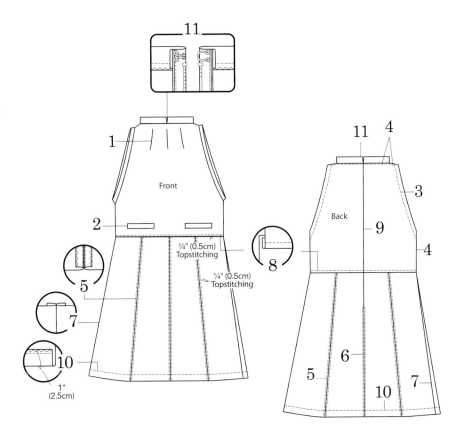

A. Stitching the Darts

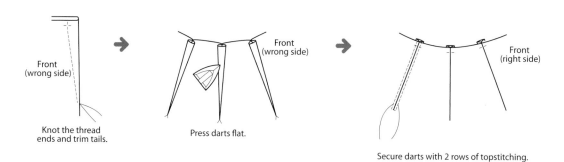

Front
(wrong side)

Front
(wrong side)

Front
(right side)

Knot the thread
ends and trim tails.

Press darts flat.

Secure darts with 2 rows of topstitching.

B. Making the Pockets

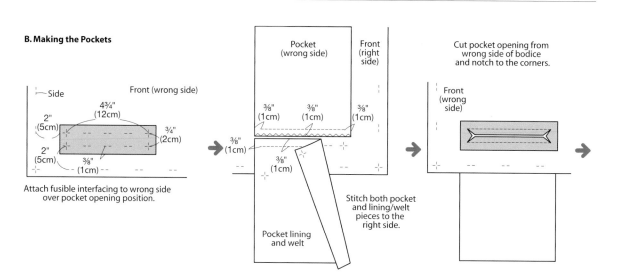

Side

Front (wrong side)

4¾"
(12cm)

2"
(5cm)

¾"
(2cm)

2"
(5cm)

⅜"
(1cm)

Attach fusible interfacing to wrong side
over pocket opening position.

Pocket
(wrong side)

Front
(right
side)

⅜"
(1cm)

⅜"
(1cm)

⅜"
(1cm)

⅜"
(1cm)

⅜"
(1cm)

Pocket lining
and welt

Stitch both pocket
and lining/welt
pieces to the
right side.

Cut pocket opening from
wrong side of bodice
and notch to the corners.

Front
(wrong
side)

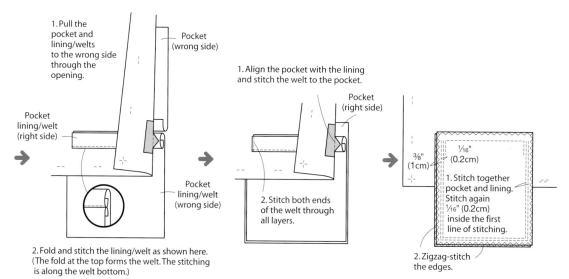

1. Pull the
pocket and
lining/welts
to the wrong side
through the
opening.

Pocket
(wrong side)

Pocket
lining/welt
(right side)

Pocket
lining/welt
(wrong side)

2. Fold and stitch the lining/welt as shown here.
(The fold at the top forms the welt. The stitching
is along the welt bottom.)

1. Align the pocket with the lining
and stitch the welt to the pocket.

Pocket
(right side)

2. Stitch both ends
of the welt through
all layers.

⅜"
(1cm)

1/16"
(0.2cm)

1. Stitch together
pocket and lining.
Stitch again
1/16" (0.2cm)
inside the first
line of stitching.

2. Zigzag-stitch
the edges.

C. Finishing the Neckline and Armholes

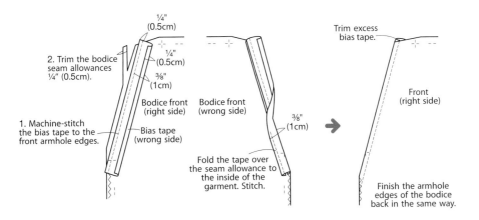

2. Trim the bodice seam allowances ¼" (0.5cm).

¼" (0.5cm)

¼" (0.5cm)

⅜" (1cm)

1. Machine-stitch the bias tape to the front armhole edges.

Bodice front (right side)

Bodice front (wrong side)

Bias tape (wrong side)

⅜" (1cm)

Fold the tape over the seam allowance to the inside of the garment. Stitch.

Trim excess bias tape.

Front (right side)

Finish the armhole edges of the bodice back in the same way.

D. Stitching the Bodice Side Seams

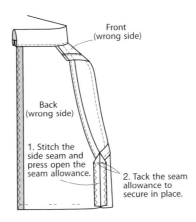

Front (wrong side)

Back (wrong side)

1. Stitch the side seam and press open the seam allowance.

2. Tack the seam allowance to secure in place.

E. Attaching the Hook-and-Eye Closure

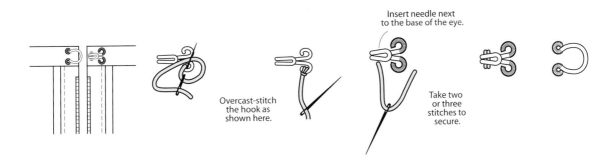

Overcast-stitch the hook as shown here.

Insert needle next to the base of the eye.

Take two or three stitches to secure.

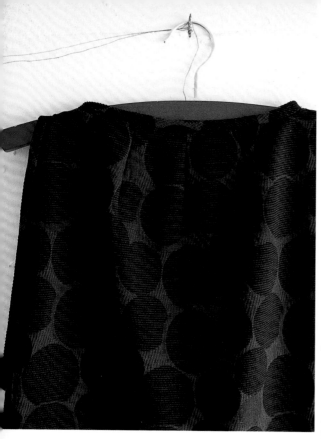

8 I Am Baby Bateau

(shown on pages 12–13)

Materials

Fabric: 67" x 56" (170 cm x 142 cm) of dot-print jacquard-woven fabric

Fusible interfacing: 19¾" x 11¾" (50 cm x 30 cm)

Invisible zipper: 27½" (70 cm) long

Hook and eye: 1 set

Optional Sizing Adjustments

For the most accurate fit, use the metric version of all measurements and sizing adjustments.

★ a = H / 16

★ b = H / 16 + 1½" (4 cm)

★ c = H / 4

★ d = H / 8

H = Hip measurement

Seam Allowances

Unless otherwise noted, seam allowances are ⅜" (1 cm).

● Fabric Layout

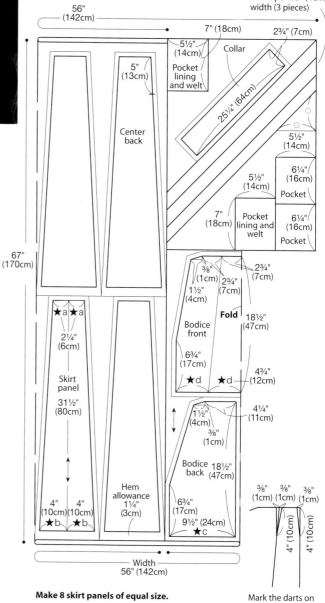

Make 8 skirt panels of equal size.

Mark the darts on the bodice front.

Construction Steps

1. Stitch darts in bodice pieces (A).

2. Make the two pockets (B).

3. Stitch the shoulder seams and bodice side seams and press open seam allowances (C).

4. Finish the neckline and armholes (D).

5. Zigzag-stitch the raw edges of the skirt panels. Join the four skirt front panels. Join the two skirt back panels. Press open all of the seam allowances.

6. Stitch the center back up to the zipper opening.

7. Stitch the skirt side seams and press open the seam allowances.

8. Attach the skirt to the bodice. Topstitch.

9. Install the invisible zipper as shown on page 74.

10. Sew the hem, zigzag-stitching the raw edge.

11. Attach the hook-and-eye closure as shown on page 59.

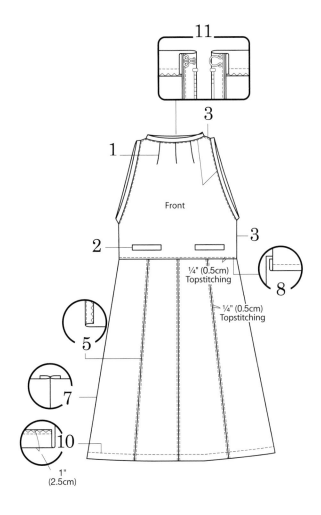

A. Stitching the Darts

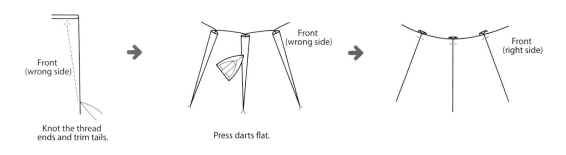

Front
(wrong side)

Knot the thread
ends and trim tails.

Front
(wrong side)

Press darts flat.

Front
(right side)

B. Making the Pockets

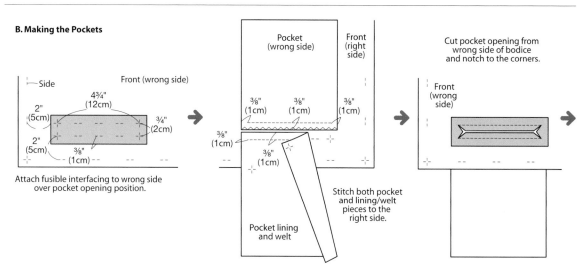

Side

Front (wrong side)

4¾"
(12cm)

2"
(5cm)

¾"
(2cm)

2"
(5cm)

⅜"
(1cm)

Attach fusible interfacing to wrong side
over pocket opening position.

Pocket
(wrong side)

Front
(right
side)

⅜"
(1cm)

⅜"
(1cm)

⅜"
(1cm)

⅜"
(1cm)

⅜"
(1cm)

Pocket lining
and welt

Stitch both pocket
and lining/welt
pieces to the
right side.

Cut pocket opening from
wrong side of bodice
and notch to the corners.

Front
(wrong
side)

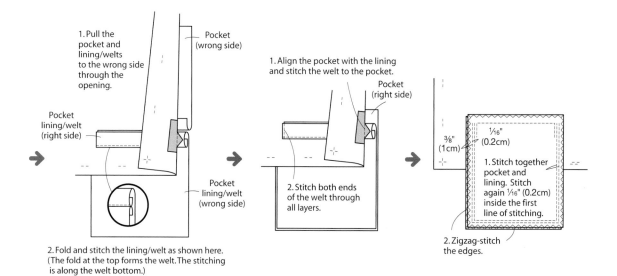

1. Pull the
pocket and
lining/welts
to the wrong side
through the
opening.

Pocket
(wrong side)

Pocket
lining/welt
(right side)

Pocket
lining/welt
(wrong side)

2. Fold and stitch the lining/welt as shown here.
(The fold at the top forms the welt. The stitching
is along the welt bottom.)

1. Align the pocket with the lining
and stitch the welt to the pocket.

Pocket
(right side)

2. Stitch both ends
of the welt through
all layers.

⅜"
(1cm)

1⁄16"
(0.2cm)

1. Stitch together
pocket and
lining. Stitch
again 1⁄16" (0.2cm)
inside the first
line of stitching.

2. Zigzag-stitch
the edges.

C. Stitching the Shoulders and Bodice Side Seams

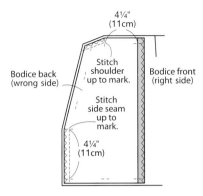

4¼"
(11cm)

Bodice back
(wrong side)

Stitch
shoulder
up to mark.

Bodice front
(right side)

Stitch
side seam
up to
mark.

4¼"
(11cm)

D. Finishing the Neckline and Armholes

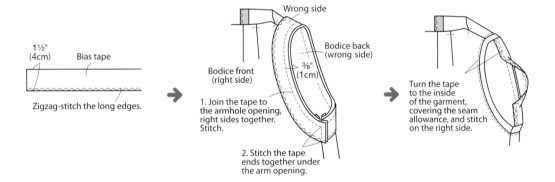

1½"
(4cm)   Bias tape

Zigzag-stitch the long edges.

Wrong side

Bodice back
(wrong side)

⅜"
(1cm)

Bodice front
(right side)

1. Join the tape to
the armhole opening,
right sides together.
Stitch.

2. Stitch the tape
ends together under
the arm opening.

Turn the tape
to the inside
of the garment,
covering the seam
allowance, and stitch
on the right side.

9 I Am Sassy Sundress

(shown on page 14)

Materials

Fabric: 110¼" x 44¾" (280 cm x 114 cm) of glitter-printed cotton lawn

Fusible interfacing: 1¼" x 2¼" (3 cm x 6 cm)

Optional Sizing Adjustments

For the most accurate fit, use the metric version of all measurements and sizing adjustments.

Seam Allowances

Unless otherwise noted, seam allowances are ⅜" (1 cm).

● **Fabric Layout**

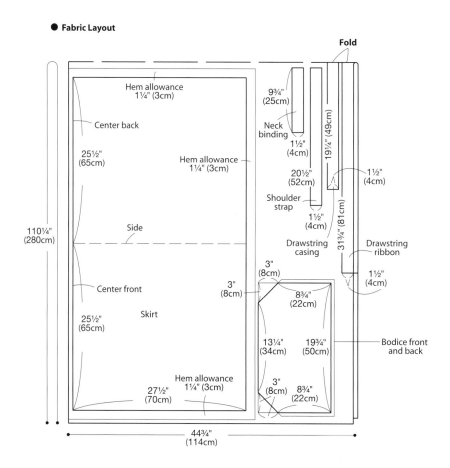

Construction Steps

1. Bind the upper edge of the bodice (A).

2. Attach the shoulder straps (B).

3. Stitch the bodice side seams (C). Press seam allowances to back.

4. Attach the drawstring casing (D).

5. Join the skirt panels. Hem all sides (E).

6. Attach skirt to bodice (F).

7. Make the drawstring ribbon and insert it into casing (G).

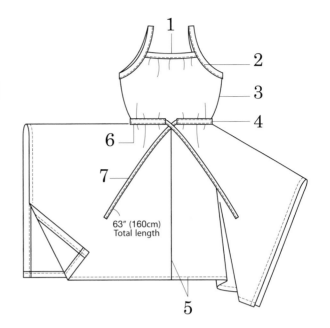

63" (160cm)
Total length

A. Making the Bodice Binding

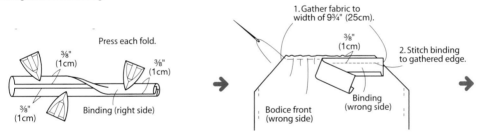

Press each fold.

⅜" (1cm)

⅜" (1cm)

⅜" (1cm)

Binding (right side)

1. Gather fabric to width of 9¾" (25cm).

⅜" (1cm)

2. Stitch binding to gathered edge.

Binding (wrong side)

Bodice front (wrong side)

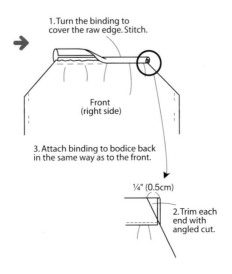

1. Turn the binding to cover the raw edge. Stitch.

Front (right side)

3. Attach binding to bodice back in the same way as to the front.

¼" (0.5cm)

2. Trim each end with angled cut.

B. Attaching the Shoulder Straps

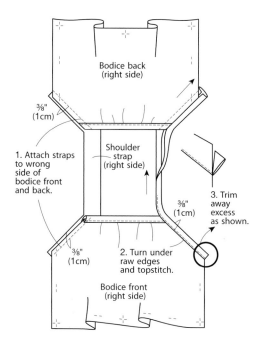

Bodice back
(right side)

³⁄₈"
(1cm)

1. Attach straps
to wrong
side of
bodice front
and back.

Shoulder
strap
(right side)

³⁄₈"
(1cm)

3. Trim
away
excess
as shown.

³⁄₈"
(1cm)

2. Turn under
raw edges
and topstitch.

Bodice front
(right side)

C. Stitching the Bodice Side Seams

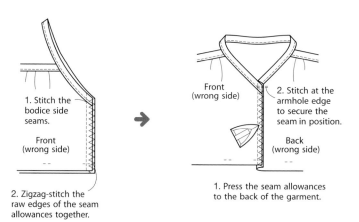

1. Stitch the
bodice side
seams.

Front
(wrong side)

2. Zigzag-stitch the
raw edges of the seam
allowances together.

Front
(wrong side)

2. Stitch at the
armhole edge
to secure the
seam in position.

Back
(wrong side)

1. Press the seam allowances
to the back of the garment.

D. Attaching the Drawstring Casing

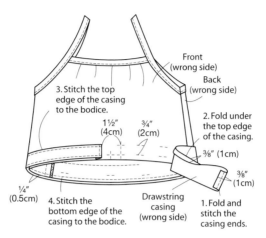

Front
(wrong side)

Back
(wrong side)

3. Stitch the top
edge of the casing
to the bodice.

2. Fold under
the top edge
of the casing.

1½"
(4cm)

¾"
(2cm)

⅜" (1cm)

⅜"
(1cm)

¼"
(0.5cm)

4. Stitch the
bottom edge of the
casing to the bodice.

Drawstring
casing
(wrong side)

1. Fold and
stitch the
casing ends.

E. Making the Skirt

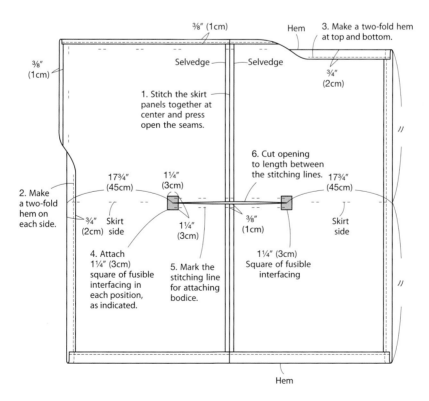

⅜" (1cm)

Hem

3. Make a two-fold hem
at top and bottom.

Selvedge

Selvedge

⅜"
(1cm)

¾"
(2cm)

1. Stitch the skirt
panels together at
center and press
open the seams.

6. Cut opening
to length between
the stitching lines.

17¾"
(45cm)

17¾"
(45cm)

1¼"
(3cm)

2. Make
a two-fold
hem on
each side.

¾"   Skirt
(2cm) side

1¼"
(3cm)

⅜"
(1cm)

Skirt
side

4. Attach
1¼" (3cm)
square of fusible
interfacing in
each position,
as indicated.

5. Mark the
stitching line
for attaching
bodice.

1¼" (3cm)
Square of fusible
interfacing

Hem

F. Attaching Bodice and Skirt

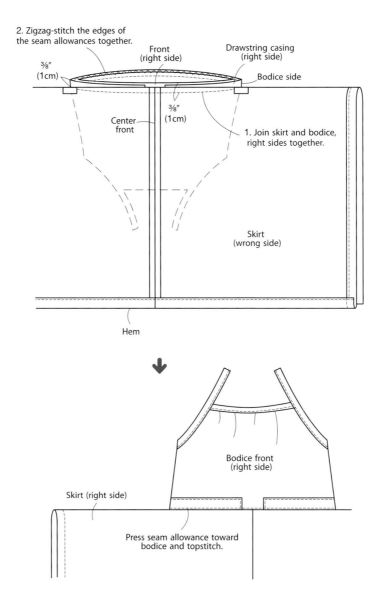

2. Zigzag-stitch the edges of
the seam allowances together.

Front
(right side)

Drawstring casing
(right side)

⅜"
(1cm)

Bodice side

Center
front

⅜"
(1cm)

1. Join skirt and bodice,
right sides together.

Skirt
(wrong side)

Hem

Skirt (right side)

Bodice front
(right side)

Press seam allowance toward
bodice and topstitch.

G. Making the Drawstring Ribbon

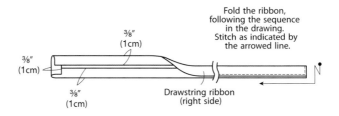

⅜"
(1cm)

Fold the ribbon,
following the sequence
in the drawing.
Stitch as indicated by
the arrowed line.

⅜"
(1cm)

⅜"
(1cm)

Drawstring ribbon
(right side)

10 I Am Twice As Nice

(shown on page 15)

Materials

Fabric: 23¾" x 51¼" (60 cm x 130 cm) of black fabric; 70¾" x 43¼" (180 cm x 110 cm) of black-and-white floral-print cotton-linen fabric

Lining: 67" x 36¼" (170 cm x 92 cm) of cupro rayon (such as Bemberg Cupro)

Optional Sizing Adjustments

For the most accurate fit, use the metric version of all measurements and sizing adjustments.

★ a = B / 4

B = Bust measurement

Seam Allowances

Unless otherwise noted, seam allowances are ⅜" (1 cm).

● **Fabric Layout**

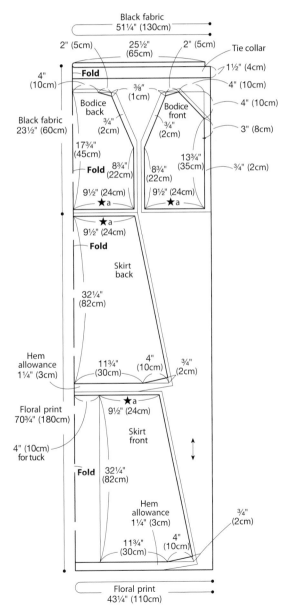

Construction Steps

1. Stitch the bodice pieces at center front.

2. Stitch the shoulder seams and press open seam allowances.

3. Attach the tie collar (A).

4. Stitch the bodice side seams and press open seam allowances. Finish armhole edges.

5. Stitch the skirt side seams and hem (B).

6. Stitch the lining side seams and hem (C).

7. Stitch the skirt and lining at the waist. Join the skirt and bodice (D).

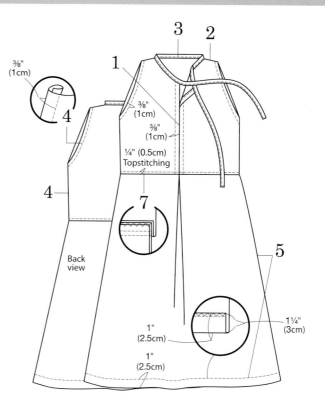

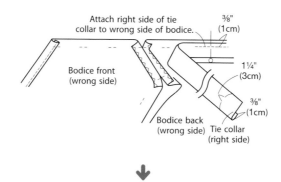

A. Attaching the Tie Collar

Attach right side of tie collar to wrong side of bodice.

Bodice front (wrong side)

Bodice back (wrong side)

Tie collar (right side)

³⁄₈" (1cm)

1¼" (3cm)

³⁄₈" (1cm)

Turn the tie collar to the right side of the garment, enclosing seam allowance. Stitch as indicated by arrowed line.

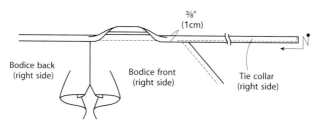

Bodice back (right side)

Bodice front (right side)

Tie collar (right side)

³⁄₈" (1cm)

B. Stitching the Skirt

1. Baste the center tuck.

4"
(10cm)

2. Stitch the side seams. Press open the seam allowances.

Skirt front
(wrong side)

3. Zigzag-stitch the raw edge of the hem. Then turn up hem and stitch.

1¼"
(3cm)

1"
(2.5cm)

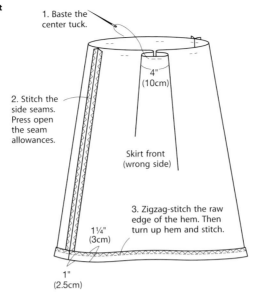

C. Stitching the Lining

⅜"
(1cm)

1. Stitch the lining side seams.

Lining
(wrong side)

31¼"
(79.5cm)

⅜"
(1cm)

⅝"
(1.5cm)

2. Hem the lining, folding under the raw edges.

⅜"
(1cm)

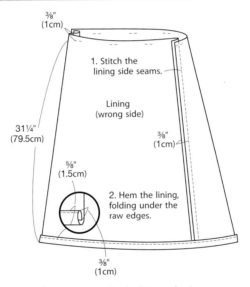

Use the same pattern for the lining as for the skirt front. Cut waist and side, allowing each ⅜" (1cm) of seam allowance. Leave no allowance for the hem.

D. Joining Skirt, Lining, and Bodice

Bodice
(right side)

Skirt (wrong side)

Lining
(right side)

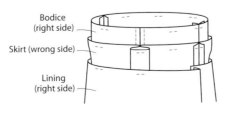

Assemble the three pieces, as shown, and stitch to attach at waist.

11 I Am Tiny Tucks

(shown on pages 16–17)

Materials

Fabric: 106¼" x 35½" (270 cm x 90 cm) of gabardine

Fusible interfacing: 2¼" x 13¾" (6 cm x 35 cm)

Invisible zipper: 23½" (60 cm) long

Hook and eye: 1 set

Cutwork beads: 51

Optional Sizing Adjustments

For the most accurate fit, use the metric version of all measurements and sizing adjustments.

★ a = H / 4 + ¾" (2 cm)

★ b = H / 4 + 2¼" (6 cm)

H = Hip measurement

Seam Allowances

Unless otherwise noted, seam allowances are ⅜" (1 cm).

● **Fabric Layout**

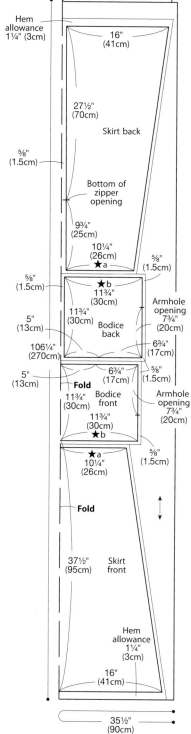

Hem allowance 1¼" (3cm)

16" (41cm)

27½" (70cm)

Skirt back

⅝" (1.5cm)

Bottom of zipper opening

9¾" (25cm)

10¼" (26cm) ★a

⅝" (1.5cm)

⅝" (1.5cm)

★b
11¾" (30cm)

Armhole opening 7¾" (20cm)

11¾" (30cm)

5" (13cm)

Bodice back

106¼" (270cm)

6¾" (17cm)

5" (13cm)

6¾" (17cm)

⅝" (1.5cm)

Fold

11¾" (30cm)

Bodice front

Armhole opening 7¾" (20cm)

11¾" (30cm) ★b

★a
10¼" (26cm)

⅝" (1.5cm)

Fold

37½" (95cm)

Skirt front

Hem allowance 1¼" (3cm)

16" (41cm)

35½" (90cm)

Construction Steps

1. Stitch shoulder seams and press open seam allowances. Stitch bodice side seams and sleeve hems (A).

2. Stitch skirt side seams. Press open seam allowances.

3. Attach bodice and skirt. Topstitch.

4. Stitch center back to zipper opening. Install zipper (B).

5. Finish neckline (C).

6. Zigzag-stitch the raw edge and stitch hem.

7. Install hook-and-eye closure as shown on page 59.

8. Stitch beads onto bodice and around the armhole edges (D).

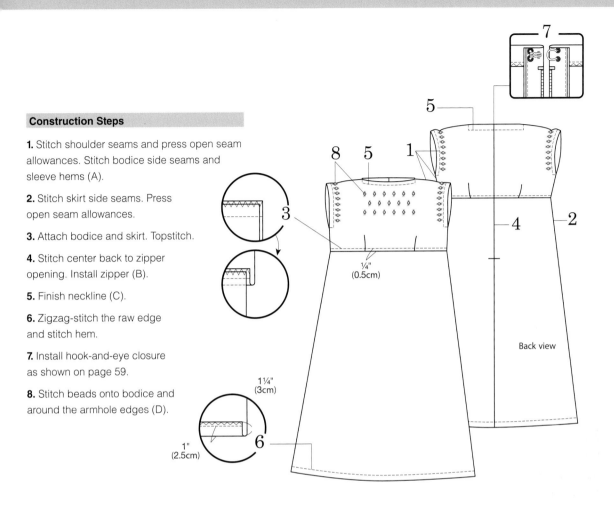

Back view

A. Making the Bodice

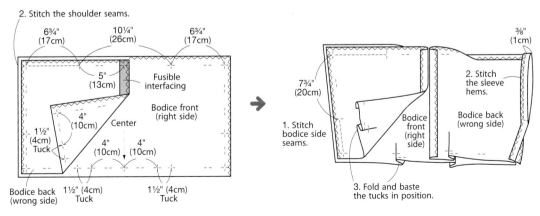

2. Stitch the shoulder seams.

1. Mark the bodice front and back for tucking.

B. Installing the Zipper

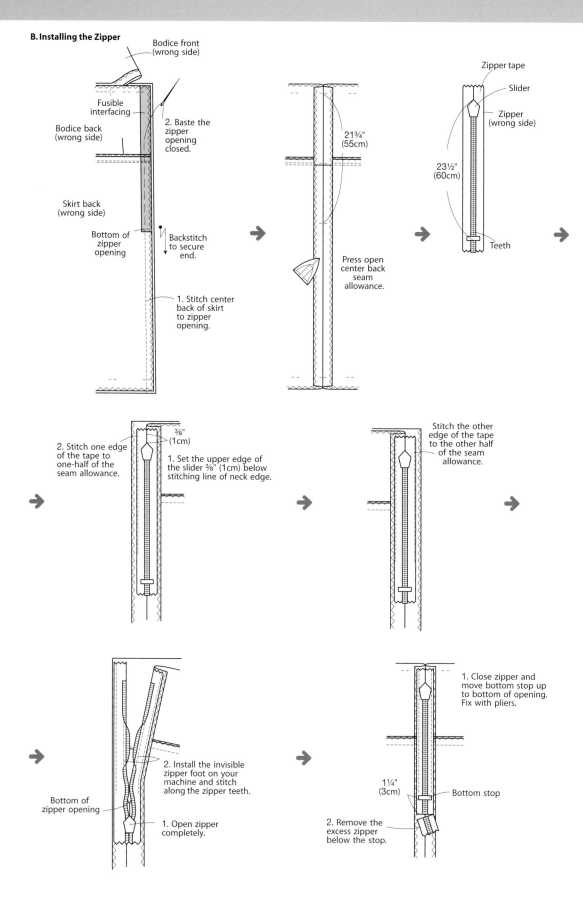

Bodice front
(wrong side)

Fusible
interfacing

Bodice back
(wrong side)

2. Baste the
zipper
opening
closed.

Skirt back
(wrong side)

Bottom of
zipper
opening

Backstitch
to secure
end.

1. Stitch center
back of skirt
to zipper
opening.

21¾"
(55cm)

Press open
center back
seam
allowance.

Zipper tape

Slider

Zipper
(wrong side)

23½"
(60cm)

Teeth

2. Stitch one edge
of the tape to
one-half of the
seam allowance.

⅜"
(1cm)

1. Set the upper edge of
the slider ⅜" (1cm) below
stitching line of neck edge.

Stitch the other
edge of the tape
to the other half
of the seam
allowance.

2. Install the invisible
zipper foot on your
machine and stitch
along the zipper teeth.

Bottom of
zipper opening

1. Open zipper
completely.

1. Close zipper and
move bottom stop up
to bottom of opening.
Fix with pliers.

1¼"
(3cm)

Bottom stop

2. Remove the
excess zipper
below the stop.

C. Finishing the Neckline

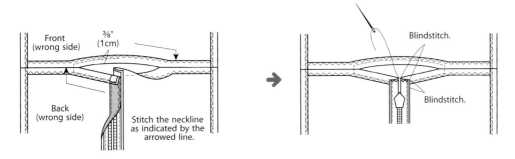

Front (wrong side)

⅜" (1cm)

Back (wrong side)

Stitch the neckline as indicated by the arrowed line.

Blindstitch.

Blindstitch.

D. Positioning and Stitching the Beads

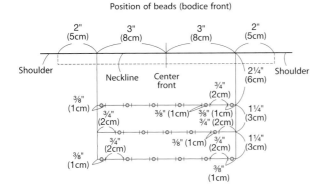

Position of beads (bodice front)

2" (5cm)   3" (8cm)   3" (8cm)   2" (5cm)

Shoulder   Shoulder

Neckline   Center front

2¼" (6cm)

¾" (2cm)

⅜" (1cm)   ¾" (2cm)   ⅜" (1cm)   ⅜" (1cm)   ¾" (2cm)

1¼" (3cm)

¾" (2cm)   ⅜" (1cm)   ¾" (2cm)

1¼" (3cm)

⅜" (1cm)

⅜" (1cm)

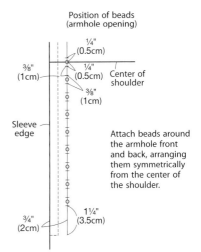

Position of beads (armhole opening)

¼" (0.5cm)

⅜" (1cm)

¼" (0.5cm)   Center of shoulder

⅜" (1cm)

Sleeve edge

Attach beads around the armhole front and back, arranging them symmetrically from the center of the shoulder.

¾" (2cm)

1¼" (3.5cm)

● Beading Sequence

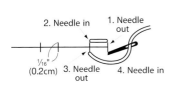

2. Needle in   1. Needle out

1/16" (0.2cm)   3. Needle out   4. Needle in

Pull thread to create tucks.

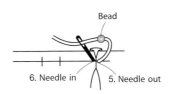

Bead

6. Needle in   5. Needle out

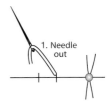

1. Needle out

Repeat Steps 1 through 6 to attach all the beads.

12 I Am Raglan to Riches

(shown on pages 18–19)

Materials

Fabric: 45" x 59" (114 cm x 150 cm) of thread-dyed plaid gauze

Trim: 63" (160 cm) length of ⅜" (1 cm) lace.

Optional Sizing Adjustments

For the most accurate fit, use the metric version of all measurements and sizing adjustments.

Seam Allowances

Unless otherwise noted, seam allowances are ⅜" (1 cm).

● **Fabric Layout**

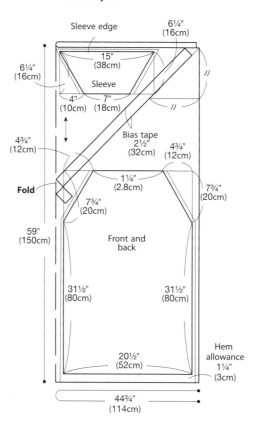

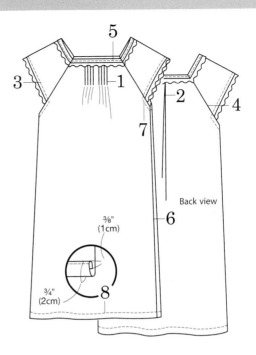

Back view

Construction Steps

1. Stitch the tucks on the dress front (A).

2. Stitch the tucks on the dress back (B).

3. Attach the lace trim to the sleeve edges (C).

4. Attach the sleeves to the body (D).

5. Trim the neckline with lace (E).

6. Stitch the dress side seams (F).

7. Finish the arm openings (G).

8. Enclose the raw edge and stitch the hem.

A. Stitching Front Tucks

Space and mark tucks symmetrically from center front.

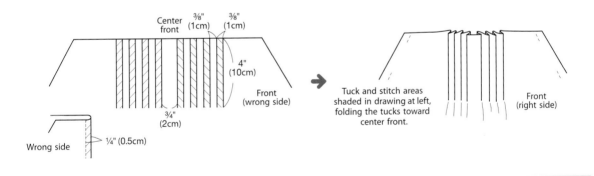

Tuck and stitch areas shaded in drawing at left, folding the tucks toward center front.

B. Stitching Back Tucks

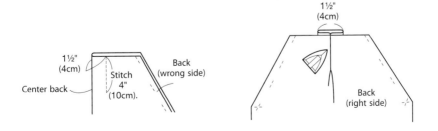

C. Trimming the Sleeves

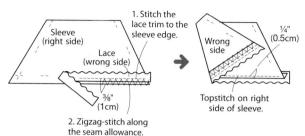

Sleeve (right side)

Lace (wrong side)

1. Stitch the lace trim to the sleeve edge.

2. Zigzag-stitch along the seam allowance.

⅜" (1cm)

Wrong side

¼" (0.5cm)

Topstitch on right side of sleeve.

D. Attaching Sleeves to Body

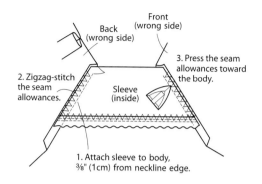

Front (wrong side)

Back (wrong side)

2. Zigzag-stitch the seam allowances.

3. Press the seam allowances toward the body.

Sleeve (inside)

1. Attach sleeve to body, ⅜" (1cm) from neckline edge.

E. Trimming the Neckline

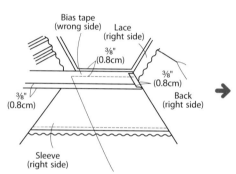

Bias tape (wrong side)

Lace (right side)

⅜" (0.8cm)

⅜" (0.8cm)

⅜" (0.8cm)

Back (right side)

Sleeve (right side)

Attach lace to right side of neck edge at front and back and also to right side of tops of sleeves. Stitch bias tape along entire neckline.

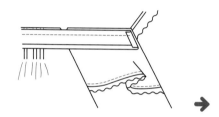

To stitch the corner, raise the presser foot with the needle in the fabric. Fold and flatten the fabric away from the needle. Then lower the foot and stitch.

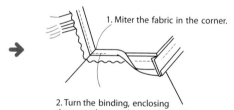

1. Miter the fabric in the corner.

2. Turn the binding, enclosing the raw edges, and topstitch in place.

F. Stitching the Side Seams

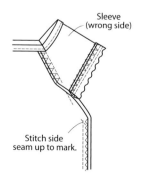

Sleeve (wrong side)

Stitch side seam up to mark.

G. Finishing the Arm Openings

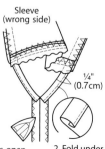

Sleeve (wrong side)

¼" (0.7cm)

1. Press open the side seam.

2. Fold under raw edge, turn under seam allowance, and stitch around the arm opening. Press.

13 I Am All the Trimmings

(shown on pages 18–19)

Materials

Fabric: 59" x 74¾" (150 cm x 190 cm) of mellow lace or other textured knit

Elastic tape: 14¼" (36 cm) length of ⅜" (1 cm) tape.

Optional Sizing Adjustments

For the most accurate fit, use the metric version of all measurements and sizing adjustments.

Seam Allowances

Unless otherwise noted, seam allowances are ⅜" (1 cm).

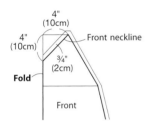

● **Fabric Layout**

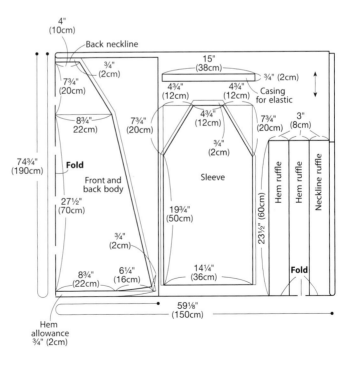

Construction Steps

1. Finish the raw edges of all ruffles with zigzag stitch (A). Zigzag-stitch the bottom edge of the sleeves.

2. Add the elastic to the sleeve cuffs and attach the sleeves to the dress body (B).

3. Finish the neckline and attach the ruffle (C).

4. Stitch the dress side seams and underarm seams (D).

5. Hem the dress and attach the ruffle.

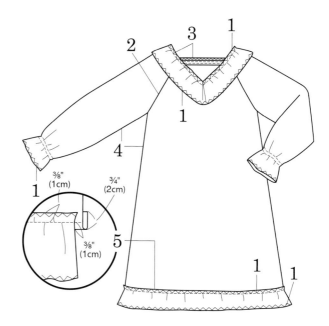

A. Finishing the Ruffle Edges

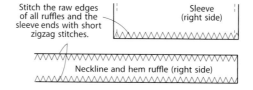

Stitch the raw edges of all ruffles and the sleeve ends with short zigzag stitches.

Sleeve (right side)

Neckline and hem ruffle (right side)

B. Attaching the Sleeves

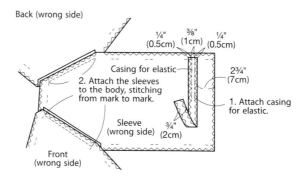

Back (wrong side)

¼" (0.5cm) ⅜" (1cm) ¼" (0.5cm)

Casing for elastic

2¾" (7cm)

2. Attach the sleeves to the body, stitching from mark to mark.

1. Attach casing for elastic.

Sleeve (wrong side) ¾" (2cm)

Front (wrong side)

C. Finishing the Neckline

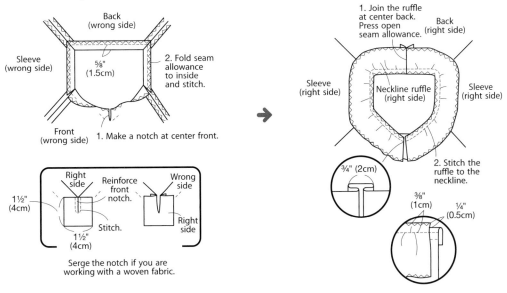

Back
(wrong side)

Sleeve
(wrong side)

⅝"
(1.5cm)

2. Fold seam
allowance
to inside
and stitch.

Front
(wrong side)

1. Make a notch at center front.

1½"
(4cm)

Right
side

Reinforce
front
notch.

Wrong
side

Stitch.

Right
side

1½"
(4cm)

Serge the notch if you are
working with a woven fabric.

1. Join the ruffle
at center back.
Press open
seam allowance.

Back
(right side)

Sleeve
(right side)

Neckline ruffle
(right side)

Sleeve
(right side)

¾" (2cm)

2. Stitch the
ruffle to the
neckline.

⅜"
(1cm)

¼"
(0.5cm)

D. Stitching the Side and Underarm Seams

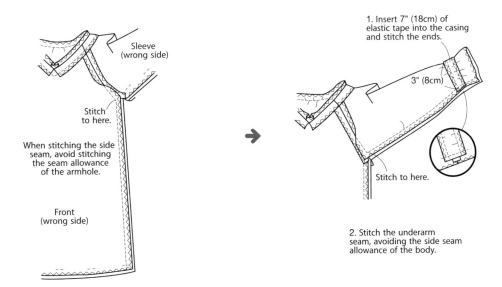

Sleeve
(wrong side)

Stitch
to here.

When stitching the side
seam, avoid stitching
the seam allowance
of the armhole.

Front
(wrong side)

1. Insert 7" (18cm) of
elastic tape into the casing
and stitch the ends.

3" (8cm)

Stitch to here.

2. Stitch the underarm
seam, avoiding the side seam
allowance of the body.

14 I Am All Wrapped Up

(shown on page 19)

Materials

Fabric: 94½" x 47¼" (240 cm x 120 cm) of crinkle-finish linen gauze

Optional Sizing Adjustments

For the most accurate fit, use the metric version of all measurements and sizing adjustments.

★ a = H / 4

★ b = H / 4 + ¾" (2 cm)

H = Hip measurement

Seam Allowances

Unless otherwise noted, seam allowances are ⅜" (1 cm).

● **Fabric Layout**

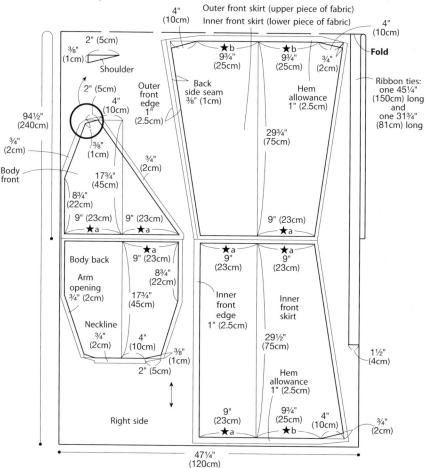

Outer front skirt (upper piece of fabric)
Inner front skirt (lower piece of fabric)

4" (10cm)

4" (10cm)

Fold

Ribbon ties: one 45¼" (150cm) long and one 31¾" (81cm) long

★b 9¾" (25cm)

★b 9¾" (25cm)

¾" (2cm)

Hem allowance 1" (2.5cm)

29¾" (75cm)

9" (23cm)

★a

2" (5cm)

⅜" (1cm)

Shoulder

2" (5cm)

4" (10cm)

Outer front edge 1" (2.5cm)

Back side seam ⅜" (1cm)

94½" (240cm)

¾" (2cm)

Body front

⅜" (1cm)

¾" (2cm)

17¾" (45cm)

8¾" (22cm)

9" (23cm)

9" (23cm)

★a

★a

Body back

Arm opening ¾" (2cm)

Neckline ¾" (2cm)

★a 9" (23cm)

8¾" (22cm)

17¾" (45cm)

4" (10cm)

⅜" (1cm)

2" (5cm)

★a 9" (23cm)

★a 9" (23cm)

Inner front edge 1" (2.5cm)

Inner front skirt

29½" (75cm)

Hem allowance 1" (2.5cm)

1½" (4cm)

Right side

9" (23cm)

★a

9¾" (25cm)

★b

4" (10cm)

¾" (2cm)

47¼" (120cm)

Construction Steps

1. Stitch shoulder seams and bodice side seams (A).

2. Finish the arm openings.

3. Finish back neckline.

4. Sew the right side seam, making the opening for the drawstring at the waist (B).

5. Hem the skirt.

6. Attach the skirt to the bodice and topstitch.

7. Make the ribbon ties.

8. Finish the front neckline and the front skirt edges, enclosing one end of each ribbon tie in a hemmed edge at the waistline (C).

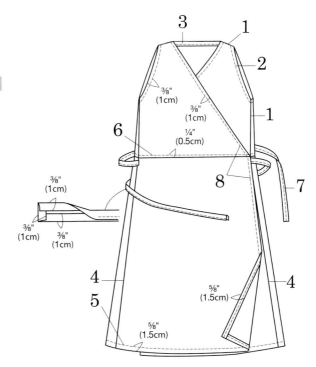

A. Stitching the Shoulder and Side Seams

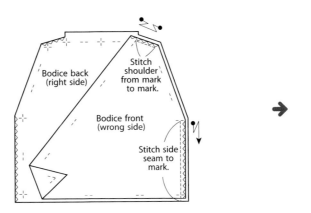

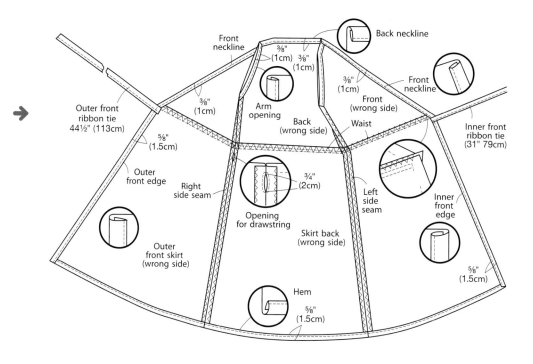

Back neckline

Front
neckline

⅜"
(1cm)   ⅜"
(1cm)

Front
neckline

⅜"
(1cm)

Front
(wrong side)

⅜"
(1cm)

Arm
opening

Back
(wrong side)

Waist

Outer front
ribbon tie
44½" (113cm)

Inner front
ribbon tie
(31" 79cm)

⅝"
(1.5cm)

Outer
front edge

Right
side seam

Left
side
seam

Inner
front
edge

Opening
for drawstring

¾"
(2cm)

Skirt back
(wrong side)

Outer
front skirt
(wrong side)

⅝"
(1.5cm)

Hem

⅝"
(1.5cm)

⅝"
(1.5cm)

B. Making the Drawstring Opening

You can use this technique to make the opening for a drawstring or for making buttonholes. The length of the hole depends on the width of the drawstring or on the diameter and the thickness of the button.

Stitch width
¹⁄₁₆" (0.1cm)
Short stitch

Stitch width
⅛" (0.4cm)
0 stitch

Stitch width
¹⁄₁₆" (0.1cm)
Short stitch

Stitch width
⅛" (0.4cm)
0 stitch

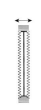

Cut center
to create
opening.

C. Attaching the Ribbon Ties

Ribbon tie

Finish the edges
of the skirt fronts,
enclosing one end
of each ribbon tie in
a hemmed edge.

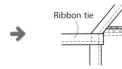

Ribbon tie

Fold ribbon
ties to the outside
of dress and
stitch to secure
in place.

15 I Am Dainty Drops

(shown on page 20)

Materials

Fabric: 94½" x 42½" (240 cm x 108 cm) of dobby seersucker

Fusible interfacing: 23½" x 19¾" (60 cm x 50 cm)

Optional Sizing Adjustments

For the most accurate fit, use the metric version of all measurements and sizing adjustments.

★ a = H / 2

★ b = H / 4

★ c = H / 8

★ d = H / 2 + 21¼" (54 cm)

H = Hip measurement

Seam Allowances

Unless otherwise noted, seam allowances are ⅜" (1 cm).

● **Fabric Layout**

Cap sleeve

5" (13cm)   5" (13cm)   4" (10cm)

5½" (14cm)

4" (10cm)

6¼" (16cm)

4" (10cm)

8¾" (22cm)

6¼" (16cm)

7¾" (20cm)

5½" (14cm)

Bodice

8¾" (22cm)

7" (18cm)   7" (18cm)

7¾" (20cm)

19¾" (50cm)

Bodice facing

★a

1¼" (3cm)   1¼" (3cm)

94½" (240cm)

Skirt

25½" (65cm)

Hem allowance 1¼" (3.5cm)

41" (104cm)

42½" (108cm)

Construction Steps

1. Stitch cap sleeves (A).

2. Stitch bodice side seams.

3. Attach sleeves to the bodice (B).

4. Attach the bodice facing (C).

5. Topstitch bodice and armhole edges.

6. Stitch side seams of skirt. Attach skirt and bodice and topstitch waist.

7. Fold and stitch raw edges of hem. Turn up hem and stitch.

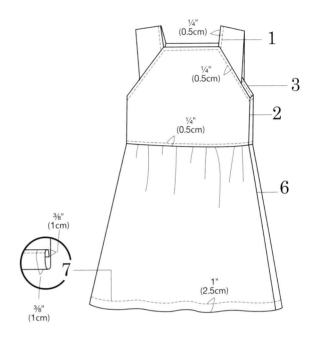

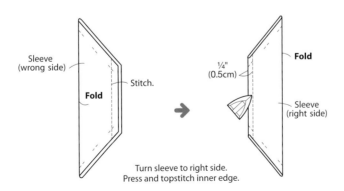

A. Making the Cap Sleeves

Sleeve (wrong side)

Fold

Stitch.

¼" (0.5cm)

Fold

Sleeve (right side)

Turn sleeve to right side.
Press and topstitch inner edge.

B. Attaching the Sleeves to the Bodice

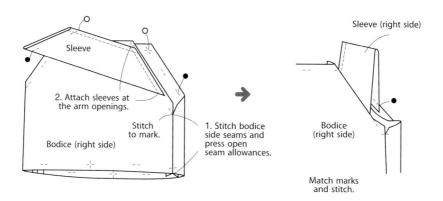

Sleeve

2. Attach sleeves at the arm openings.

Stitch to mark.

1. Stitch bodice side seams and press open seam allowances.

Bodice (right side)

Sleeve (right side)

Bodice (right side)

Match marks and stitch.

C. Attaching the Facing

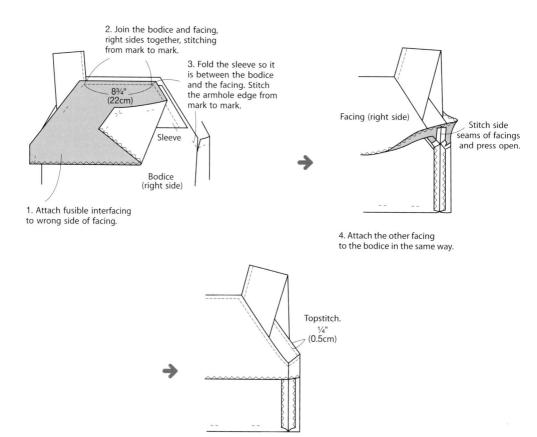

2. Join the bodice and facing, right sides together, stitching from mark to mark.

3. Fold the sleeve so it is between the bodice and the facing. Stitch the armhole edge from mark to mark.

8¾" (22cm)

Sleeve

Bodice (right side)

1. Attach fusible interfacing to wrong side of facing.

Facing (right side)

Stitch side seams of facings and press open.

4. Attach the other facing to the bodice in the same way.

Topstitch. ¼" (0.5cm)

16 I Am Cute Contrast

(shown on page 21)

Materials

Fabric: 74¾" x 59" (190 cm x 150 cm) of striped linen fabric

Fusible interfacing: 23½" x 19¾" (60 cm x 50 cm)

Optional Sizing Adjustments

For the most accurate fit, use the metric version of all measurements and sizing adjustments.

★ a = H / 2

★ b = H / 4

★ c = H / 8

★ d = H / 2 + 21¼" (54 cm)

H = Hip measurement

Seam Allowances

Unless otherwise noted, seam allowances are ⅜" (1 cm).

● **Fabric Layout**

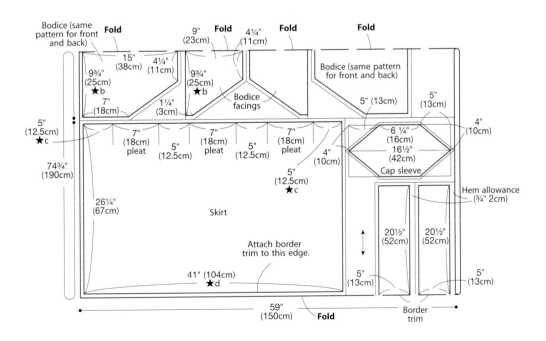

Construction Steps

1. Stitch cap sleeves (A).

2. Stitch bodice side seams.

3. Attach sleeves to the bodice (B).

4. Attach facing and topstitch (C). Attach border to lower edge of skirt and topstitch.

5. Form pleats in skirt.

6. Stitch side seams of skirt.

7. Attach skirt and bodice.Topstitch.

8. Attach border to lower edge of skirt and topstitch. Hem border with two-fold hem.

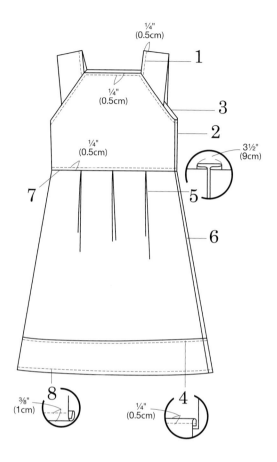

A. Making the Cap Sleeves

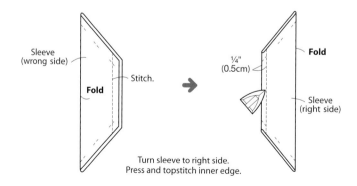

Sleeve (wrong side)

Fold

Stitch.

¼" (0.5cm)

Fold

Sleeve (right side)

Turn sleeve to right side.
Press and topstitch inner edge.

B. Attaching the Sleeves to the Bodice

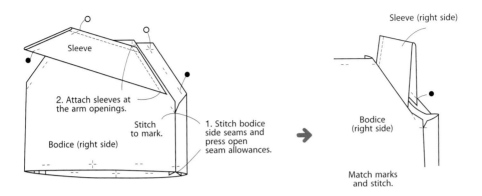

Sleeve

2. Attach sleeves at the arm openings.

Stitch to mark.

1. Stitch bodice side seams and press open seam allowances.

Bodice (right side)

Sleeve (right side)

Bodice (right side)

Match marks and stitch.

C. Attaching the Facing

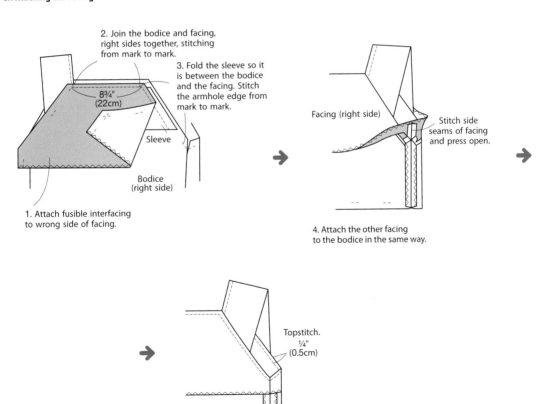

2. Join the bodice and facing, right sides together, stitching from mark to mark.

3. Fold the sleeve so it is between the bodice and the facing. Stitch the armhole edge from mark to mark.

8¾" (22cm)

Sleeve

Bodice (right side)

1. Attach fusible interfacing to wrong side of facing.

Facing (right side)

Stitch side seams of facing and press open.

4. Attach the other facing to the bodice in the same way.

Topstitch. ¼" (0.5cm)

17

I Am Sweetly Tied

(shown on page 22)

● **Fabric Layout**

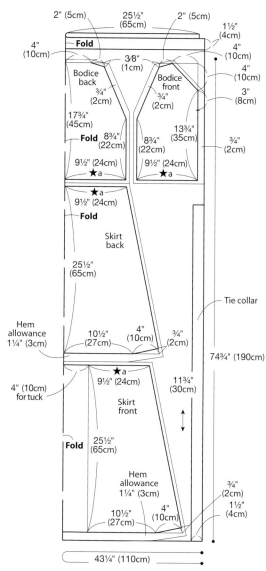

Materials

Fabric: 74¾" x 43¼" (190 cm x 110 cm) of small-floral-print fabric

Optional Sizing Adjustments

For the most accurate fit, use the metric version of all measurements and sizing adjustments.

★ a = B / 4

B = Bust measurement

Seam Allowances

Unless otherwise noted, seam allowances are ⅜" (1 cm).

Construction Steps

1. Stitch the bodice pieces at center front.

2. Stitch the shoulder seams and press open seam allowances.

3. Attach the tie collar (A).

4. Stitch the bodice side seams and press open seam allowances. Finish armhole edges.

5. Stitch the skirt side seams and hem (B).

6. Attach the skirt and bodice at waistline. Topstitch.

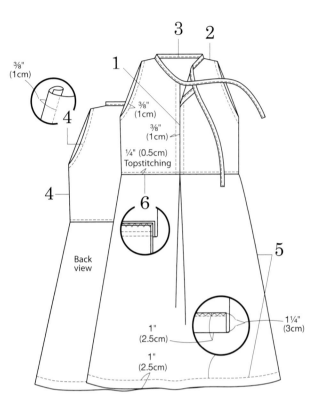

³⁄₈" (1cm)

³⁄₈" (1cm)

³⁄₈" (1cm)

¼" (0.5cm) Topstitching

Back view

1" (2.5cm)

1" (2.5cm)

1¼" (3cm)

A. Attaching the Tie Collar

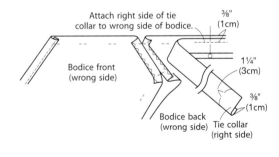

Attach right side of tie collar to wrong side of bodice.

³⁄₈" (1cm)

Bodice front (wrong side)

1¼" (3cm)

³⁄₈" (1cm)

Bodice back (wrong side) Tie collar (right side)

Turn the tie collar to the right side of garment, enclosing seam allowance. Stitch as indicated by arrowed line.

³⁄₈" (1cm)

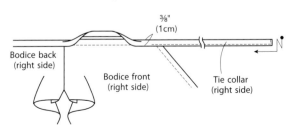

Bodice back (right side)

Bodice front (right side)

Tie collar (right side)

B. Stitching the Skirt Side Seams

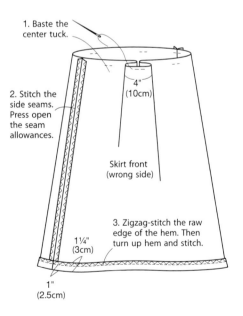

1. Baste the center tuck.

2. Stitch the side seams. Press open the seam allowances.

4" (10cm)

Skirt front (wrong side)

3. Zigzag-stitch the raw edge of the hem. Then turn up hem and stitch.

1¼" (3cm)

1" (2.5cm)

18 I Am Tripled Tier

(shown on page 23)

Materials

Fabric: 67" x 42½" (170 cm x 108 cm) of dobby voile

Trim: 7½ yd. (6.8 m) length of ¾" (2 cm) lace

Optional Sizing Adjustments

For the most accurate fit, use the metric version of all measurements and sizing adjustments.

★ a = H / 2 + ¾" (2 cm)

H = Finished hip measurement

Seam Allowances

Unless otherwise noted, seam allowances are ⅜" (1 cm).

● **Fabric Layout**

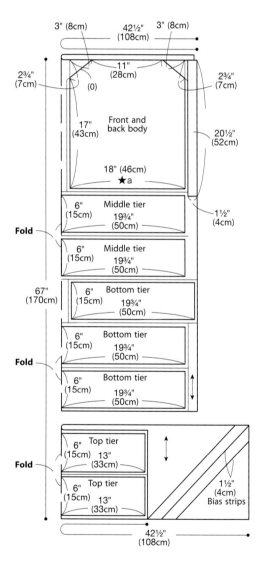

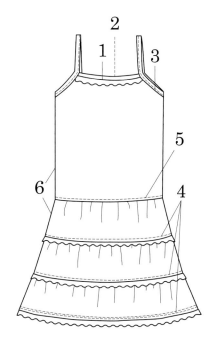

Construction Steps

1. Attach lace to front neckline (A).
Cover edge with bias strips.

2. Cover upper edge of back body
with bias strips.

3. Attach shoulder straps as shown
on page 66.

4. Attach lace to skirt tiers and assemble
the tiers for skirt front and back (B).

5. Attach the skirt to the dress body.

6. Stitch the dress side seams (C).

A. Attaching Lace to Neckline

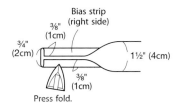

Bias strip
(right side)
³⁄₈" (1cm)
³⁄₄" (2cm)
1½" (4cm)
³⁄₈" (1cm)
Press fold.

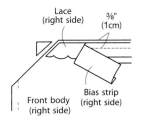

Lace
(right side)
³⁄₈" (1cm)
Front body
(right side)
Bias strip
(right side)

Cover edge of back neckline
with bias strip in same way,
without adding lace.

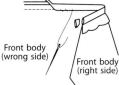

Cover edge with bias
strip and blindstitch.

Front body
(wrong side)
Front body
(right side)

B. Assembling the Skirt

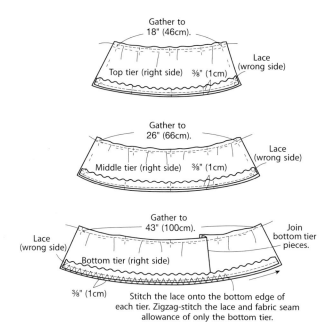

Gather to 18" (46cm).

Top tier (right side) ⅜" (1cm)

Lace (wrong side)

Gather to 26" (66cm).

Middle tier (right side) ⅜" (1cm)

Lace (wrong side)

Gather to 43" (100cm).

Lace (wrong side)

Bottom tier (right side)

Join bottom tier pieces.

⅜" (1cm) Stitch the lace onto the bottom edge of each tier. Zigzag-stitch the lace and fabric seam allowance of only the bottom tier.

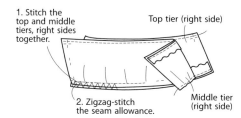

1. Stitch the top and middle tiers, right sides together.

Top tier (right side)

2. Zigzag-stitch the seam allowance.

Middle tier (right side)

3. Stitch the middle and bottom tiers together in the same way.

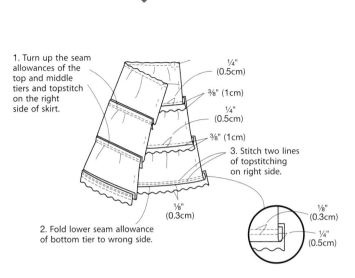

1. Turn up the seam allowances of the top and middle tiers and topstitch on the right side of skirt.

¼" (0.5cm)

⅜" (1cm)

¼" (0.5cm)

⅜" (1cm)

3. Stitch two lines of topstitching on right side.

⅛" (0.3cm)

2. Fold lower seam allowance of bottom tier to wrong side.

⅛" (0.3cm)

¼" (0.5cm)

C. Stitching the Side Seams

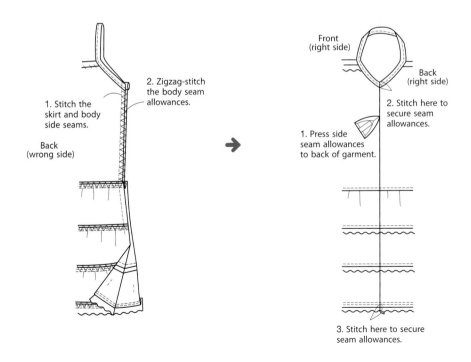

2. Zigzag-stitch the body seam allowances.

1. Stitch the skirt and body side seams.

Back (wrong side)

Front (right side)

Back (right side)

2. Stitch here to secure seam allowances.

1. Press side seam allowances to back of garment.

3. Stitch here to secure seam allowances.

19

I Am Jumper for Joy

(shown on pages 24–25)

● **Fabric Layout**

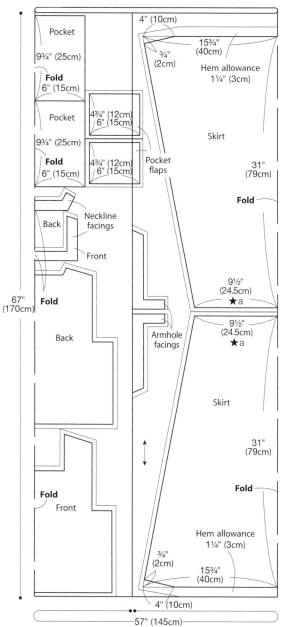

Materials

Fabric: 67" x 57½" (170 cm x 146 cm) of nylon tussah or yarn-dyed twill

Fusible interfacing: 35½" x 11¾" (90 cm x 30 cm)

Optional Sizing Adjustments

For the most accurate fit, use the metric version of all measurements and sizing adjustments.

★ a = H / 4

H = Finished hip measurement

Seam Allowances

Unless otherwise noted, seam allowances are ⅜" (1 cm).

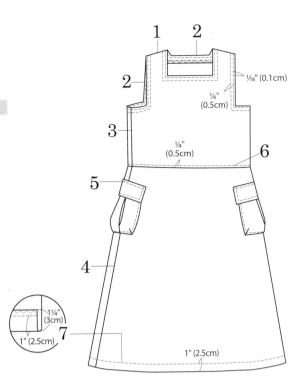

1 2

1/16" (0.1cm)

1/4" (0.5cm)

1/4" (0.5cm)

2

3

5

6

4

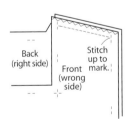

1¼" (3cm)

1" (2.5cm) 7

1" (2.5cm)

Construction Steps

1. Stitch shoulder seams (A).

2. Attach the facings to the neckline and arm openings (B).

3. Stitch the bodice side seams (C).

4. Stitch the skirt side seams.

5. Attach the pockets (D).

6. Attach the skirt to the bodice.

7. Zigzag-stitch the raw edge and sew the hem.

● **Making the Front and Back Bodice**

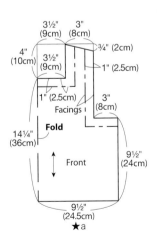

3½" (9cm)   3" (8cm)

4" (10cm)   3½" (9cm)   ¾" (2cm)

1" (2.5cm)

1" (2.5cm)   3" (8cm)
Facings

14¼" (36cm)   **Fold**

Front   9½" (24cm)

9½" (24.5cm)
★a

Copy outline of
front body for facings,
redrawing the neckline
for the back facing.

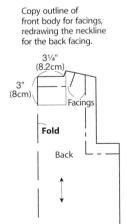

3¼" (8.2cm)

3" (8cm)   Facings

Fold

Back

A. Stitching the Shoulder Seams

Back (right side)   Stitch up to mark.

Front (wrong side)

B. Attaching the Facings

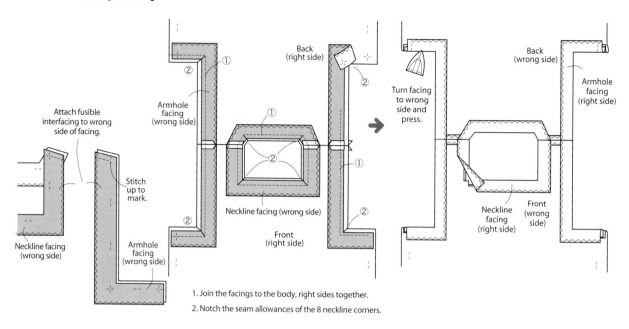

Attach fusible interfacing to wrong side of facing.

Stitch up to mark.

Neckline facing (wrong side)

Armhole facing (wrong side)

Armhole facing (wrong side)

Back (right side)

Neckline facing (wrong side)

Front (right side)

Turn facing to wrong side and press.

Back (wrong side)

Armhole facing (right side)

Neckline facing (right side)

Front (wrong side)

1. Join the facings to the body, right sides together.
2. Notch the seam allowances of the 8 neckline corners.

C. Stitching the Bodice Side Seams

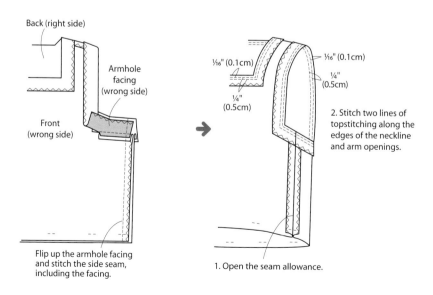

Back (right side)

Armhole facing (wrong side)

Front (wrong side)

Flip up the armhole facing and stitch the side seam, including the facing.

1/16" (0.1cm)

1/4" (0.5cm)

1/16" (0.1cm)

1/4" (0.5cm)

1. Open the seam allowance.

2. Stitch two lines of topstitching along the edges of the neckline and arm openings.

D. Making the Pockets

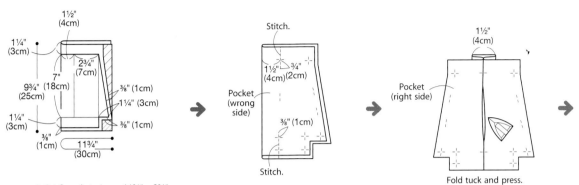

1¼"
(3cm)

1½"
(4cm)

2¾"
(7cm)

7"

9¾"
(25cm)

⅜" (1cm)

1¼" (3cm)

1¼"
(3cm)

⅜" (1cm)

⅜"
(1cm)

11¾"
(30cm)

Stitch.

1½"   ¾"
(4cm) (2cm)

Pocket
(wrong
side)

⅜" (1cm)

Stitch.

Pocket
(right side)

1½"
(4cm)

Fold tuck and press.

1. Cut 2 pocket pieces, 11¾" x 9¾"
(30cm x 25cm), and mark as shown.

2. Remove shaded area.

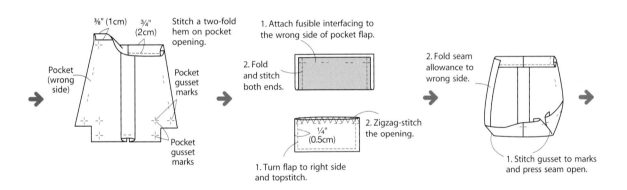

⅜" (1cm)   ¾"
(2cm)

Stitch a two-fold
hem on pocket
opening.

Pocket
(wrong
side)

Pocket
gusset
marks

Pocket
gusset
marks

1. Attach fusible interfacing to
the wrong side of pocket flap.

2. Fold
and stitch
both ends.

¼"
(0.5cm)

2. Zigzag-stitch
the opening.

1. Turn flap to right side
and topstitch.

2. Fold seam
allowance to
wrong side.

1. Stitch gusset to marks
and press seam open.

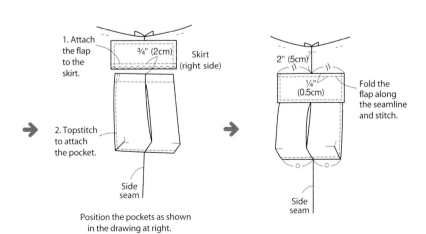

1. Attach
the flap
to the
skirt.

¾" (2cm)

Skirt
(right side)

2. Topstitch
to attach
the pocket.

Side
seam

Position the pockets as shown
in the drawing at right.

2" (5cm)

¼"
(0.5cm)

Fold the
flap along
the seamline
and stitch.

Side
seam

20 I Am Sew Buttoned Down

(shown on pages 26–27)

Materials

Fabric: 98½" x 47¼" (250 cm x 120 cm) of lightweight herringbone wool fabric

Skirt lining: 74¾" x 36¼" (190 cm x 92 cm) of cupro rayon (such as Bemberg Cupro)

Fusible interfacing: 11¾" x 2" (30 cm x 5 cm)

Buttons: 3 matching, with 2" (5 cm) diameter

Support buttons: 3 matching, with ¼" to ⅜" (0.5 to 1cm) diameter

Optional Sizing Adjustments

For the most accurate fit, use the metric version of all measurements and sizing adjustments.

★ a = B / 4

B = Finished bust measurement

Seam Allowances

Unless otherwise noted, seam allowances are ⅜" (1 cm).

● **Fabric Layout**

Cut all bodice parts from single layer of fabric.

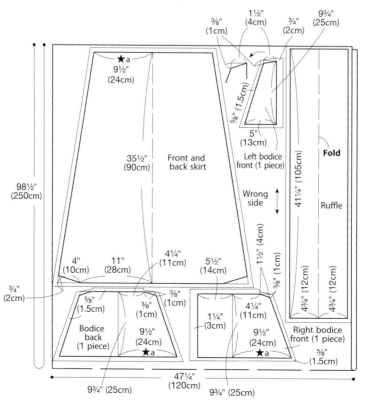

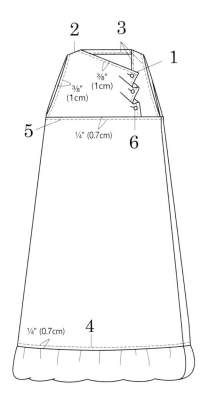

Construction Steps

1. Stitch upper edge of right front bodice (A).

2. Stitch shoulder seams (B).

3. Finish the neckline and arm openings (C).

4. Stitch the skirt and lining (D).

5. Attach the skirt to the bodice (E).

6. Make buttonholes. Attach buttons and support buttons (F).

● **Lining Layout**

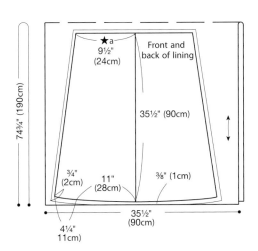

● **Positioning Buttonholes and Buttons**

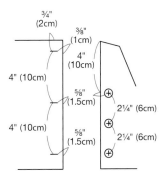

A. Finishing the Right Bodice Front Edge

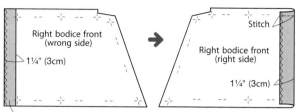

Right bodice front
(wrong side)

1¼" (3cm)

Stitch

Right bodice front
(right side)

1¼" (3cm)

Attach fusible interfacing along front edge on wrong side.
Fold to right side and stitch.

B. Stitching the Shoulder Seams

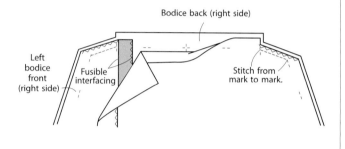

Bodice back (right side)

Left
bodice
front
(right side)

Fusible
interfacing

Stitch from
mark to mark.

C. Finishing the Neckline and Arm Openings

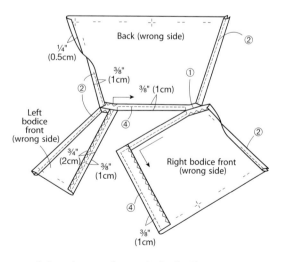

Back (wrong side)

¼"
(0.5cm)

⅜"
(1cm)

⅜" (1cm)

②

①

②

④

Left
bodice
front
(wrong side)

¾"
(2cm)

⅜"
(1cm)

Right bodice front
(wrong side)

②

④

⅜"
(1cm)

1. Open the seam allowance in the shoulders.

2. Stitch the armhole openings with a two-fold hem.

3. Stitch the edge of the left bodice front.

4. Create a continuous two-fold hem along the edges of
the neckline and the right bodice front.

D. Stitching the Skirt and Lining

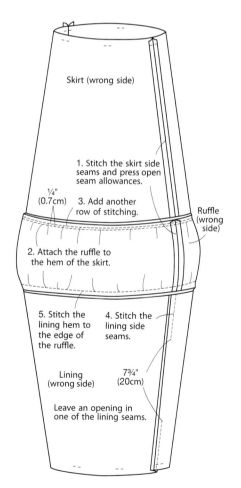

Skirt (wrong side)

1. Stitch the skirt side
seams and press open
seam allowances.

¼"
(0.7cm)

3. Add another
row of stitching.

Ruffle
(wrong
side)

2. Attach the ruffle to
the hem of the skirt.

5. Stitch the
lining hem to
the edge of
the ruffle.

4. Stitch the
lining side
seams.

Lining
(wrong side)

7¾"
(20cm)

Leave an opening in
one of the lining seams.

E. Attaching the Skirt and Bodice

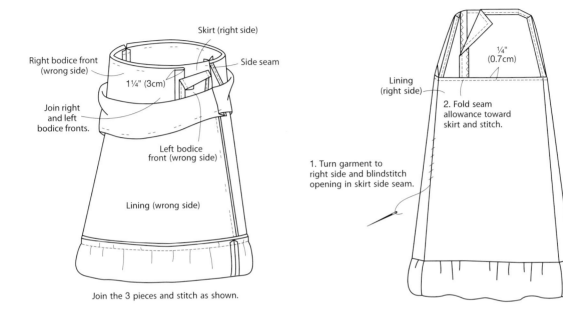

Skirt (right side)

Side seam

Right bodice front
(wrong side)

1¼" (3cm)

Join right
and left
bodice fronts.

Left bodice
front (wrong side)

Lining (wrong side)

Join the 3 pieces and stitch as shown.

Lining
(right side)

¼"
(0.7cm)

2. Fold seam
allowance toward
skirt and stitch.

1. Turn garment to
right side and blindstitch
opening in skirt side seam.

F. Attaching Support Buttons

Support buttons lessen the tension on the button closure
and are especially suited for fine, delicate fabrics. Position
a support button of about ¼" (0.5cm) diameter directly
behind the outer button and stitch through both buttons
for added stability.

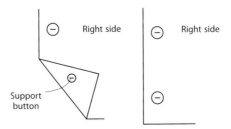

Right side

Right side

Support
button

21 I Am Shift into Tunic

(shown on pages 28–29)

Materials

Fabric: 157½" x 14¼" (400 cm x 36 cm) of kimono cloth (or other silk fabric)

Skirt lining: 51¼" x 36¼" (190 cm x 92 cm) of cupro rayon (such as Bemberg Cupro)

Fusible interfacing: 11¾" x 1¼" (30 cm x 3 cm)

Buttons: 3 matching, with ¾" (2 cm) diameter

Support buttons: 3 matching, with ¼" to ⅜" (0.5 to 1cm) diameter

Optional Sizing Adjustments

For the most accurate fit, use the metric version of all measurements and sizing adjustments.

★ $a = B / 4$

B = Finished bust measurement

Seam Allowances

Unless otherwise noted, seam allowances are ⅜" (1 cm).

● **Fabric Layout**

Prepare four 39¼" pieces of cloth 14¼" (36cm) wide. Join each pair of pieces and lay out as shown.

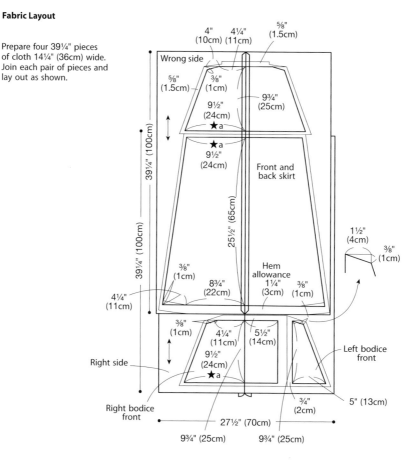

Construction Steps

1. Stitch upper edge of right front bodice (A).

2. Stitch shoulder seams (B).

3. Finish the neckline and arm openings (C).

4. Stitch and hem the skirt and lining (D).

5. Attach the skirt to the bodice (E).

6. Make buttonholes. Attach buttons and support buttons as shown on page 105.

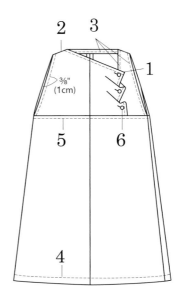

● **Lining Layout**

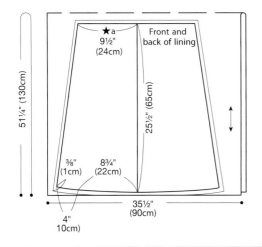

● **Positioning Buttonholes and Buttons**

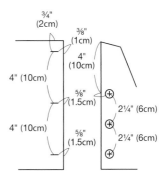

A. Finishing the Right Bodice Front Edge

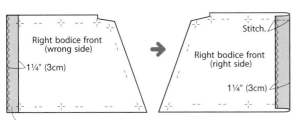

Attach fusible interfacing along front edge on wrong side.
Fold to right side and stitch.

B. Stitching the Shoulder Seams

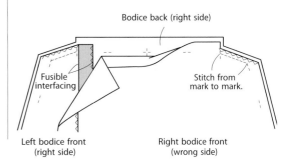

C. Finishing the Neckline and Arm Openings

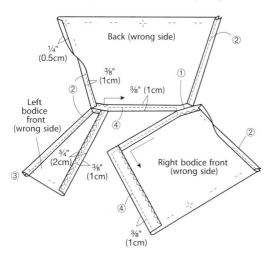

1. Open the seam allowance in the shoulders.

2. Stitch the armhole openings with a two-fold hem.

3. Stitch the edge of the left bodice front.

4. Create a continuous two-fold hem along the edges of the neckline and the right bodice front.

D. Attaching the Skirt and Lining

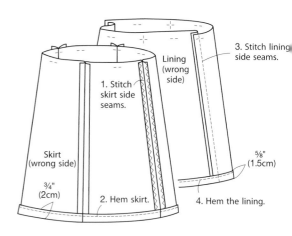

E. Attaching the Skirt and Bodice

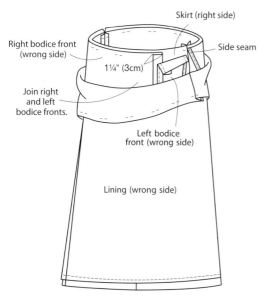

Join the 3 pieces and stitch as shown.

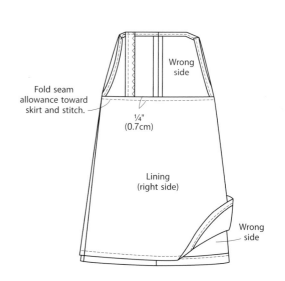

22 I Am Magical Insets

(shown on page 30)

Materials

Fabric: 70¾" x 43¼" (180 cm x 110 cm) of colorfast lawn

Double-edged lace: 39¼" (100 cm) length of 7" (18 cm) lace

Optional Sizing Adjustments

For the most accurate fit, use the metric version of all measurements and sizing adjustments.

Seam Allowances

Unless otherwise noted, seam allowances are ⅜" (1 cm).

● **Fabric Layout**

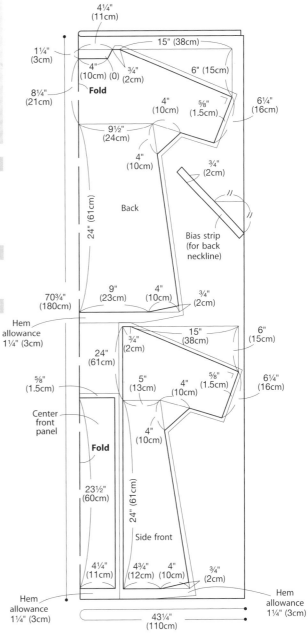

Construction Steps

1. Attach bias-strip edging to back neckline (A).

2. Attach the lace to the center front dress panel (B).

3. Attach dress fronts to center panel and finish front neckline.

4. Stitch shoulder seams.

5. Add lace to sleeve ends.

6. Stitch underarm and side seams (C).

7. Stitch two-fold hem.

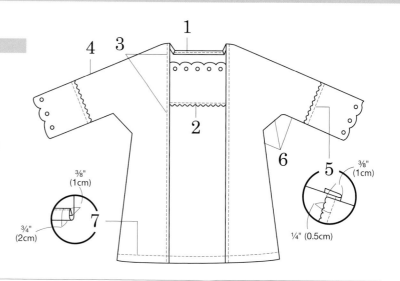

A. Edging the Back Neckline

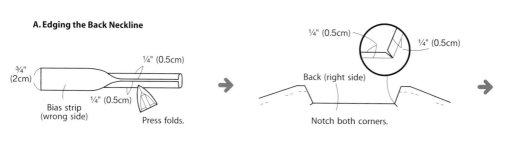

Bias strip (wrong side)

Press folds.

Back (right side)

Notch both corners.

Back (right side)

Open and notch to hold fabric straight and then attach bias tape.

Fold bias tape to the inside and stitch, mitering the corners.

B. Attaching Lace to the Center Panel

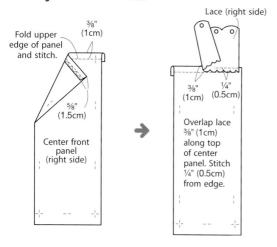

Fold upper edge of panel and stitch.

Center front panel (right side)

Lace (right side)

Overlap lace ⅜" (1cm) along top of center panel. Stitch ¼" (0.5cm) from edge.

C. Stitching Underarm and Side Seams

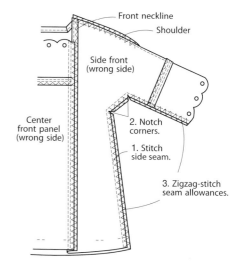

Front neckline

Shoulder

Side front (wrong side)

Center front panel (wrong side)

2. Notch corners.

1. Stitch side seam.

3. Zigzag-stitch seam allowances.

23 I Am Kimono Cut

(shown on page 31)

Materials

Fabric: 106¼" x 47¼" (270 cm x 120 cm)
of stretch corduroy; 51¼" x 19¾" (130 cm x 50 cm)
of dotted tulle

Stay tape: 51¼" (130 cm) length of ⅜" (18 cm) tape

Optional Sizing Adjustments

For the most accurate fit, use the metric version of all
measurements and sizing adjustments.

Seam Allowances

Unless otherwise noted, seam allowances
are ⅜" (1 cm).

● **Fabric Layout**

Stretch corduroy

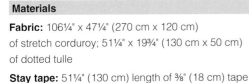

¾" (2cm)

15" (38cm)

6" (15cm)

1" (2.5cm)

9½" (24cm)

4¾" (12cm)

4" (10cm)

1" (2.5cm)

6" (15cm)

Fold

106¼" (270cm)

Front 48¼" (122.5cm)
Back 50¼" (127.5cm)

Front and
back center
panel

Front and
back side

Cut front and back center panels of tulle
in same way as stretch corduroy.

4¼" (11cm)

5" (13cm)

4" (10cm)

⅝" (1.5cm)

47¼" (120cm)

Hem allowance
1¼" (3cm)

Hem allowance
1¼" (3cm)

Construction Steps

1. Stitch the tulle to the right side of each corduroy center panel (A).

2. Stitch shoulder seams (B).

3. Attach center panels to dress side pieces (C).

4. Finish sleeve ends.

5. Stitch underarm and side seams.

6. Stitch hem.

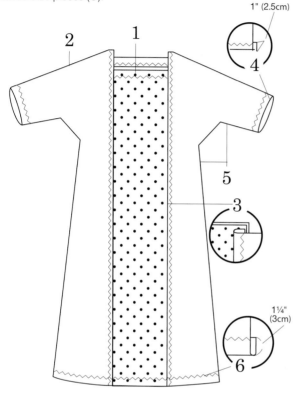

A. Stitching the Center Front and Back Panels

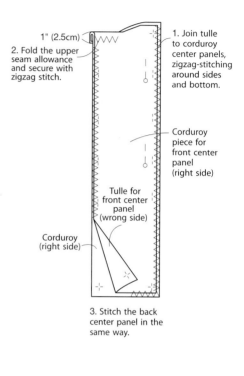

1" (2.5cm)

2. Fold the upper seam allowance and secure with zigzag stitch.

1. Join tulle to corduroy center panels, zigzag-stitching around sides and bottom.

Corduroy piece for front center panel (right side)

Tulle for front center panel (wrong side)

Corduroy (right side)

3. Stitch the back center panel in the same way.

B. Stitching the Shoulder Seams

Back side (right side)

2. Zigzag-stitch seam allowances.

Front side (wrong side)

1. Stitch.

C. Attaching Panels to Dress

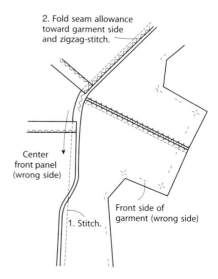

2. Fold seam allowance toward garment side and zigzag-stitch.

Center front panel (wrong side)

1. Stitch.

Front side of garment (wrong side)

24 I Am Box-Pleated Wonder

(shown on pages 32–33)

Materials

Fabric: 78¾" x 57" (200 cm x 145 cm)
of herringbone chambray

Fusible interfacing: 31½" x 19¾" (80 cm x 50 cm)

Buttons: 8 matching, with 1" (2.5 cm) diameter

Support buttons: 4 matching, with ¼" (0.5 cm) diameter

Optional Sizing Adjustments

For the most accurate fit, use the metric version of all
measurements and sizing adjustments.

Seam Allowances

Unless otherwise noted, seam allowances
are ⅜" (1 cm).

● **Fabric Layout**

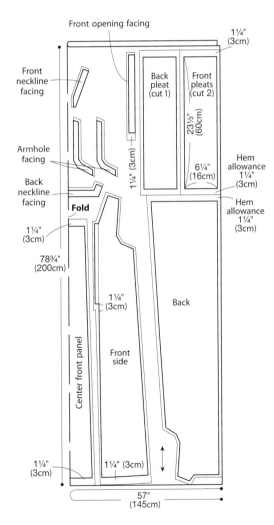

Front opening facing

Front
neckline
facing

Armhole
facing

Back
neckline
facing

Fold

1¼"
(3cm)

78¾"
(200cm)

1¼"
(3cm)

Center front panel

1¼"
(3cm)

1¼"
(3cm)

Front
side

1¼" (3cm)

1¼" (3cm)

57"
(145cm)

Back
pleat
(cut 1)

Front
pleats
(cut 2)

23½"
(60cm)

6¼"
(16cm)

1¼"
(3cm)

Hem
allowance
1¼"
(3cm)

Hem
allowance
1¼"
(3cm)

Back

Construction Steps

1. Attach skirt pleat to center back and stitch center back seam (A).

2. Position skirt pleat and stitch right front design seam and attach loops (B).

3. Stitch shoulder seams, attaching the neckline and armhole facings (C).

4. Position skirt pleat and stitch left front design seam.

5. Topstitch neckline and arm openings. Stitch side seams and facings (D).

6. Zigzag-stitch raw edge and stitch hem. Stitch along fold line of all pleats.

7. Attach buttons and support buttons as shown on page 105.

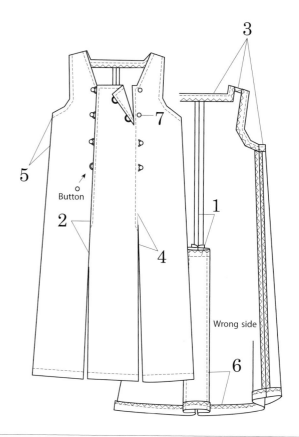

● **Positioning Loops, Pleats, and Panel**

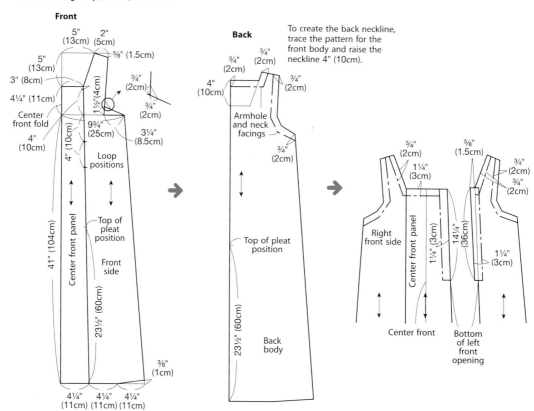

To create the back neckline, trace the pattern for the front body and raise the neckline 4" (10cm).

A. Installing the Back Pleat

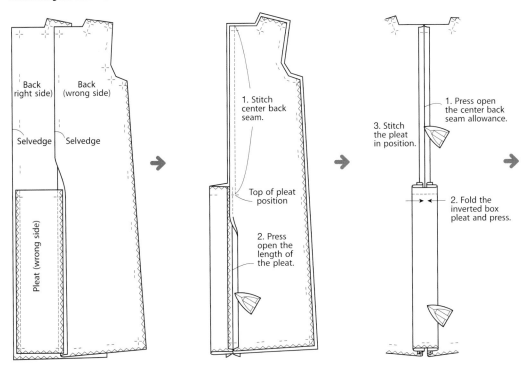

Back (right side)

Back (wrong side)

Selvedge

Selvedge

Pleat (wrong side)

1. Stitch center back seam.

Top of pleat position

2. Press open the length of the pleat.

3. Stitch the pleat in position.

1. Press open the center back seam allowance.

2. Fold the inverted box pleat and press.

● Making the Loops

Cut 8 pieces for loops to measurements shown below. (Cut with one selvedge edge to reduce risk of raveling under tension.)

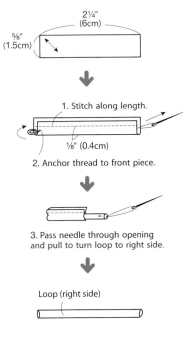

2¼" (6cm)

⅝" (1.5cm)

1. Stitch along length.

⅛" (0.4cm)

2. Anchor thread to front piece.

3. Pass needle through opening and pull to turn loop to right side.

Loop (right side)

B. Sewing Right Front Design Seam and Loops

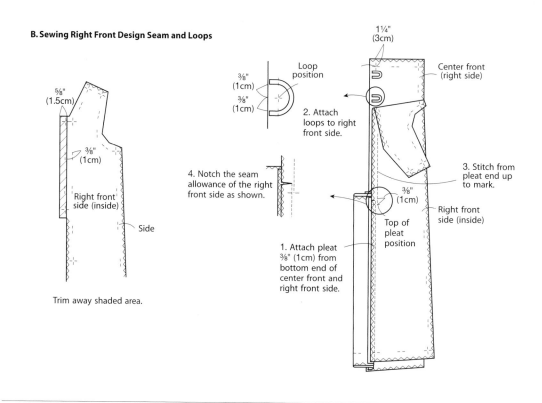

5/8"
(1.5cm)

3/8"
(1cm)

Right front
side (inside)

Side

Trim away shaded area.

3/8"
(1cm)

3/8"
(1cm)

Loop
position

2. Attach
loops to right
front side.

4. Notch the seam
allowance of the right
front side as shown.

1. Attach pleat
3/8" (1cm) from
bottom end of
center front and
right front side.

1¼"
(3cm)

Center front
(right side)

3. Stitch from
pleat end up
to mark.

3/8"
(1cm)

Right front
side (inside)

Top of
pleat
position

C. Stitching Shoulders and Facings

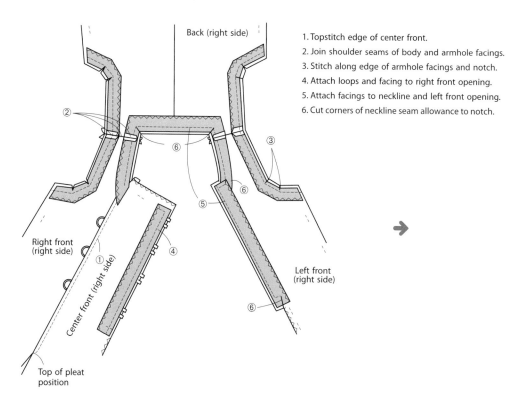

1. Topstitch edge of center front.
2. Join shoulder seams of body and armhole facings.
3. Stitch along edge of armhole facings and notch.
4. Attach loops and facing to right front opening.
5. Attach facings to neckline and left front opening.
6. Cut corners of neckline seam allowance to notch.

Back (right side)

Right front
(right side)

Center front (right side)

Left front
(right side)

Top of pleat
position

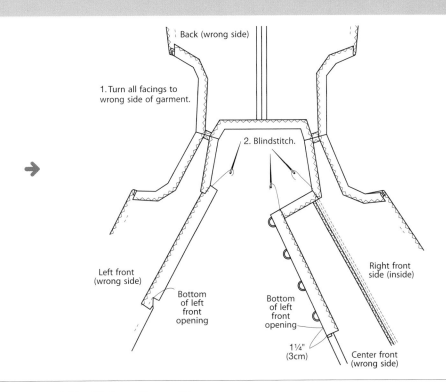

1. Turn all facings to wrong side of garment.

2. Blindstitch.

Back (wrong side)

Left front (wrong side)

Bottom of left front opening

Right front side (inside)

Bottom of left front opening

1¼" (3cm)

Center front (wrong side)

D. Stitching Side Seams, Pleats, and Hem

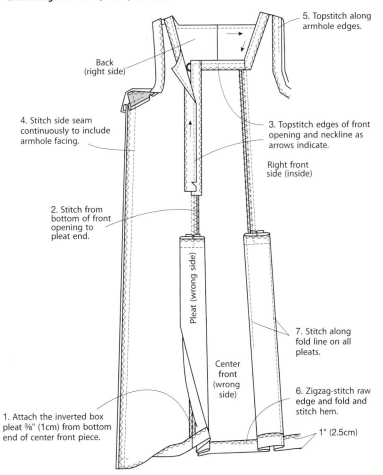

5. Topstitch along armhole edges.

Back (right side)

4. Stitch side seam continuously to include armhole facing.

3. Topstitch edges of front opening and neckline as arrows indicate.

Right front side (inside)

2. Stitch from bottom of front opening to pleat end.

Pleat (wrong side)

7. Stitch along fold line on all pleats.

Center front (wrong side)

6. Zigzag-stitch raw edge and fold and stitch hem.

1. Attach the inverted box pleat ⅜" (1cm) from bottom end of center front piece.

1" (2.5cm)

25 I Am Satin Doll

(shown on page 34)

Materials

Fabric: 67" x 45¼" (170 cm x 115 cm) of soft satin stretch fabric; 31¼" x 49¼" (80 cm x 125 cm) of raschel lace

Faux fur: Approximately 11¾" x 4" (30 cm x 10 cm)

Optional Sizing Adjustments

For the most accurate fit, use the metric version of all measurements and sizing adjustments.

★ a = B / 4

Seam Allowances

Unless otherwise noted, seam allowances are ⅜ in. (1 cm).

● **Fabric Layout**

Satin

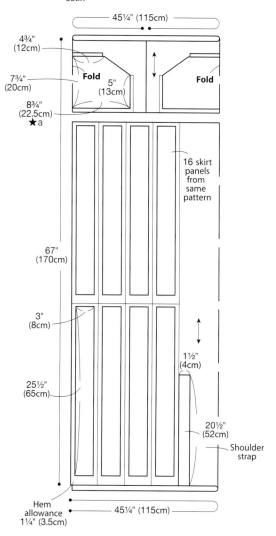

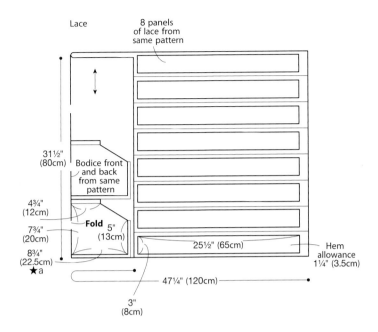

Lace

8 panels
of lace from
same pattern

31½"
(80cm)

Bodice front
and back
from same
pattern

4¾"
(12cm)

7¾"
(20cm)

Fold 5"
(13cm)

8¾"
(22.5cm)
★a

25½" (65cm)

Hem
allowance
1¼" (3.5cm)

47¼" (120cm)

3"
(8cm)

Construction Steps

1. Stitch the right side of the lace to the wrong side of the bodice along the neckline edge (A).

2. Attach the shoulder straps as shown on page 66.

3. Stitch the bodice side seams.

4. Position lace strips on 8 skirt panels (B).

5. Stitch together the skirt panels, alternating lace-covered panels with plain panels (C).

6. Gather the skirt and attach to bodice. Topstitch.

7. Fold and stitch the hem.

8. Cut the faux fur to shape (D). Attach the pieces to the tops of the shoulder straps with blindstitching.

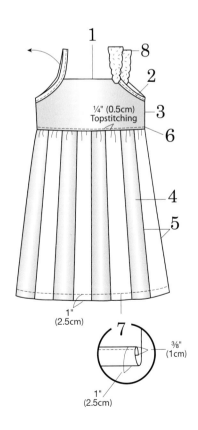

¼" (0.5cm)
Topstitching

1"
(2.5cm)

⅜"
(1cm)

1"
(2.5cm)

A. Assembling the Bodice Pieces

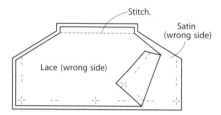

Stitch.

Satin (wrong side)

Lace (wrong side)

Turn the lace to the right side of the front bodice. Zigzag-stitch the raw edges together.

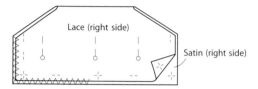

Lace (right side)

Satin (right side)

Assemble the back bodice in the same way.

B. Stitching Lace to Skirt Panels

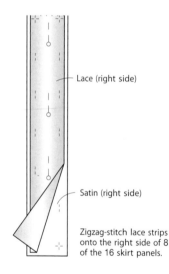

Lace (right side)

Satin (right side)

Zigzag-stitch lace strips onto the right side of 8 of the 16 skirt panels.

C. Alternating Lace and Plain Skirt Panels

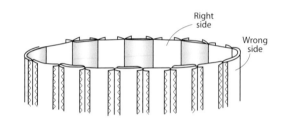

Right side

Wrong side

D. Making the Faux Fur Embellishments

Cut the pieces to make unstructured, natural shapes.

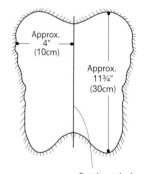

Approx. 4" (10cm)

Approx. 11¾" (30cm)

Cut through the underside to form two pieces, without cutting the fur.

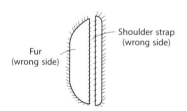

Shoulder strap (wrong side)

Fur (wrong side)

Blindstitch each piece of fur along both edges of the dress strap. Refer to the photograph on page 119 for positioning.